We Call Ourselves Disciples

SECOND EDITION

DARRELL E. JOHNSON

We Call Ourselves Disciples

SECOND EDITION

by Kenneth L. Teegarden

The Bethany Press

Saint Louis   Missouri

Library of Congress Cataloging in Publication Data

Teegarden, Kenneth L.
  We call ourselves Disciples.

  1. Christian Church (Disciples of Christ).
I. Title.
BX7321.2.T43   1983   286.6'3   82-24455
ISBN 0-8272-4215-8

Scripture quotations are from the Revised Standard Version of the Bible, copyrighted 1946, 1952 © 1971, 1972 by the Division of Christian Education, National Council of Churches of Christ in the United States of America, and are used by permission.

Cover art by Mel Lovings

Manufactured in the United States of America

Preface

I have been asked many times since my election as general minister and president to tell what the Christian Church (Disciples of Christ) is like in simple terms. *We Call Ourselves Disciples* is an attempt to do just that. It seeks to describe a movement-turned-church as it is today and to explain how it got that way. It is neither a mini-history nor a summary of doctrines and practices, but an interpretation of what the Christian Church looks like to me in 1983, and just enough of a look backward to provide perspective.

The book is intended primarily for Disciples who want to know more about the heritage, practices, beliefs, and style of operation of the Christian Church in light of developments over the last two decades. I hope that readers from other churches might gain a better understanding of who we are and why.

Obviously, it is not intended to be a definitive or authoritative statement about the Christian Church. Just how those of us who call ourselves Disciples look to me. I hope those who want to do some serious study will read *Journey in Faith: A History of the Christian Church (Disciples of Christ)* by Lester G. McAllister and William E. Tucker (Bethany Press, 1975) and *The Christian Church (Disciples of Christ): An Interpretative Examination in the Cultural Context,* edited by George G. Beazley, Jr. (Bethany Press, 1973).

I am deeply grateful to my long-time friend and colleague, James C. Suggs for his invaluable help in the research and preparation of the manuscript. He has taken time from an already crowded schedule to assist me in every way possible.

Kenneth L. Teegarden

Contents

Identity Problem

One of the apocryphal stories from conversations between the Christian Church (Disciples of Christ) and the Roman Catholic Church pokes fun at a problem we Disciples always have had. According to the yarn, the Pope, reading a report on these two-way talks, said, "I know the apostles. But who are these Disciples?"

What Disciple has not heard the same basic question? The identity of the Christian Church (Disciples of Christ) is fuzzy to a lot of people, including a good many of us who are members.

Our name doesn't help. Baptist, Methodist, Lutheran, Presbyterian, Quaker—those kinds of names communicate images, inaccurate as they may be. But "Christian Church (Disciples of Christ)"? For identification purposes, it's about as useful a name as "Political Party (American)" would be to Democrats or Republicans. In the next chapter, when I discuss origins of our brotherhood, I will explain that it was the generic, nondenominational ring of Christian Church and Disciples of Christ that appealed to the founding fathers. And in a chapter on the ideal of unity, I will point out the serviceability of such a name. At the outset, however, I am admitting what scarcely could be denied—that our name contributes to our identity problem.

For one thing, a local congregation seldom uses the Disciples of Christ as part of its spoken name. It usually is called First Christian Church or Community Christian Church or Walnut Grove Christian Church or something of the sort. Increasingly the Disciples of Christ is being included in parentheses on church signs and stationery. But there still are communities in which neither attendants at nearby service stations nor members of the

9

local Christian Church on their way to worship could direct a stranger to the Disciples Church.

In this book, I occasionally will use the full name Christian Church (Disciples of Christ). More often, I will shorten it to Christian Church or Disciples.

Also clouding our identity is use of Christian Church and similar names by other groups, some of which are almost antithetical to the Disciples. We naturally are confused with two religious bodies that shared nineteenth-century roots with the Disciples—the Church of Christ, which by the time of the 1906 United States census had gone their own way, and the independent Christian Churches, which gradually have separated themselves over the past fifty years. Even some Disciples are misled: they move to a new community and visit a Christian Church only to find that it is a congregation of another denomination.

Then a few Disciples congregations use the Church of Christ name. They naturally are mistaken for congregations of the United Church of Christ, a mainline Protestant denomination with which American Disciples are having union conversations, as well as the Churches of Christ mentioned above.

I am one of the Disciples who rebel when the Christian Church is called a sect. To me, *sect* describes an extremist splinter group, and that definitely is not how I think of our church. When I am objective, though, I can understand why an outsider could infer sectarianism from our seemingly presumptive name. I detect a tinge of defensiveness in one of the old Disciples slogans based on the name: "Not the only Christians, but Christians only."

No Standard of Orthodoxy

Our name does not deserve all of the blame for haziness about us Disciples, however.

Another reason we appear indistinct is that we have no published standard of orthodoxy. Unlike most other churches, we Disciples do not have an official doctrinal statement we can refer to when someone asks, "What does the Christian Church believe?" I will tell in other chapters why we Disciples have not been creed-writers. The point here is that when people are trying to identify a church, they tend to look for its fundamental beliefs, which usually are in print. And lacking any such propositional self-portrait, the Christian Church seems almost faceless.

Standing before a congregation of Disciples to confess faith in Jesus Christ and become part of the church, a person is asked only one question. It usually is phrased, "Do you believe that Jesus is the Christ, the Son of the living God, and do you accept him as your personal Savior?" The person who responds, "I do," might have recently completed a church membership course. If so, the instruction will not have been to transmit a system of doctrines. In fact, a person who is comfortable with a dogmatic approach would be disappointed in the Christian Church.

We Disciples have beliefs and practices in common with all sorts of Christians. These apparent similarities sometimes are superficial, sometimes fundamental. We baptize by immersion, so we look like Baptists. We have Communion every Sunday, so we look a bit like Roman Catholics. We stress the ministry of the laity, so we look a little like Quakers. Our congregations call their pastors rather than accepting assigned ministers, so in that respect we look like Presbyterians. We rely heavily on preaching and teaching, so we look somewhat like Methodists. We have congregational government, so we look a lot like the United Church of Christ. This is confusing, especially to persons who spot familiar characteristics as they transfer into the Christian Church (Disciples of Christ) from other denominations.

Cooperation, Not Competition

Still another reason we Disciples don't stand out distinctly is that we pride ourselves on cooperating with other churches. There are glaring exceptions, of course. But our usual style is to subordinate our own particular interests. We are not fierce competitors. The local Disciples pastor is not likely to proselyte (steal sheep) by claiming Christian Church superiority. In some of our regions (states or clusters of states) new congregations are established only in cooperation with other denominations. The Disciples' office of communication produces practically all of its spot announcements for television jointly with other churches. These are only random illustrations of a characteristic that softens the public image of the Christian Church (Disciples of Christ).

For these and other reasons, we who call ourselves Disciples have an identity problem. We don't intend to solve it by changing our name or adopting rigid doctrines or promoting the image of the Christian Church at the expense of the whole church. Still, we think it is important for people to know us better. Certainly members of the Christian Church need to be clear about their own corporate identity. We also are eager for outsiders at least to know how we see ourselves (I, for one, would like to know in turn what they think of us Disciples).

The purpose of this book, then, is to tell what the Christian Church (Disciples of Christ) is like in the mid-eighties. There will be enough history to provide perspective (how we got this way). But the emphasis will be on the here and now, and the future. Admittedly, all of this will be viewed through one pair of eyes—mine.

Origins

When the tiny groups that became the Christian Church (Disciples of Christ) sprang up in the first decade of the nineteenth century, they did not intend to start another denomination. In fact, that was the last thing the founders wanted. They thought of themselves as a movement to restore Christian unity on the basis of the New Testament.

Sad as it is in light of the founders' dream (I will devote a chapter to the ideal of unity), the movement became a church. And this church has contributed to the denominational mishmash in America by spinning off two additional identifiable groups.[1]

The Christian Church (Disciples of Christ) actually began as separate but similar groups in Kentucky and southwest Pennsylvania. That was America's frontier. The situation was that a church, divided to the point of ineffectiveness, was trying to evangelize a growing population that was largely unchristian. To some of the pioneers, including those who launched the Disciples movement, denominational distinctions brought from Europe seemed totally out of place in their new setting, so movements to reunite Christians emerged compulsively in scattered places among Americans pressing westward.[2]

---

1. This chapter will only sketch a broad outline of Disciples history. For details and more thorough treatment, read *Journey in Faith: A History of the Christian Church (Disciples of Christ)* by Lester G. McAllister and William E. Tucker. Bethany Press, 1975.

2. The influence of culture on the formation and development of the Disciples is dealt with at length in *The Christian Church (Disciples of Christ): An Interpretative Examination in the Cultural Context,* edited by George G. Beazley, Jr. Bethany Press, 1973.

Christians in Kentucky

Earliest of the rivulets that eventually flowed into the Disciples stream was one that welled from revivalism in Kentucky. In 1801 a tremendous camp meeting was held around the Presbyterian church at Cane Ridge, Kentucky, where Barton W. Stone was pastor. Ministers from several denominations worked together preaching the gospel to crowds estimated at 20,000. That experience of practical cooperation made a deep impression on Stone. Too, the revivalism validated a conviction of Stone and other Presbyterian ministers in the area that the Calvinist doctrine that Christ died only for the "elect" was faulty. Five preachers withdrew from the Synod of Kentucky in 1803 and organized the independent Springfield Presbytery. Less than a year later, that little presbytery was dissolved with the publication of one of the most significant documents in Disciples history, *The Last Will and Testament of the Springfield Presbytery.* Major sections of the mock will contend that the people should have "free course to the Bible," which is "the only sure guide to heaven," and that local congregations should govern themselves. First in the list is the wish "that this body die, be dissolved, and sink into union with the Body of Christ at large," a statement quoted fervently by unity-minded Disciples.

The Stone-led movement took the name Christian because it was biblical and nonsectarian. The group continued to be evangelistic and spread through the Midwest with settlers from Kentucky. Strictly congregational, the Christians were slow to develop organizations. Their so-called "conferences" were little more than rallies at which the congregations of an area could share reports. Stone's publication, the *Christian Messenger,* not only was a medium for his leadership but also served as a sort of cement among the loosely related congregations.

Disciples or Reformers

The other main Disciples tributary rose almost simultaneously in Pennsylvania near where that state meets West Virginia and Ohio. Founders were Thomas and Alexander Campbell, father and son, and their supporters, most of whom were Presbyterians (later, many Baptists were involved).

Thomas Campbell, who emigrated from Ireland to America in 1807 and sent for his family later, was disappointed to find that Presbyterians were at least as rigid and intolerant on the frontier as they had been in Ireland and Scotland. Only months after settling at Washington, Pennsylvania, he alarmed his presbytery by inviting worshipers from other branches of the Presbyterian church to take Communion with Anti-Burgher Seceder Presbyterians (his variety). Just two years after his arrival, he had been suspended by the Chartiers Presbytery and the Associate Synod of North America, and had formally withdrawn from those bodies. And during the closing months of 1809, backed by his recently formed Christian Association of Washington, Thomas wrote and published the second-oldest important document in Disciples history, the *Declaration and Address*. That statement of principles reflects the Christian Association's and Campbell's views that sectarianism is evil and that Christian unity would be possible if Christians would recognize the supreme authority of the Scriptures. It contains a key proposition still used as a summary of Disciples' convictions about the unity of the church:

That the church of Christ upon earth is essentially, intentionally, and constitutionally one; consisting of all those in every place that profess their faith in Christ and obedience to him in all things according to the scriptures, and that manifest the same by their tempers and conduct, and of none else, as none else can be truly and properly called christians.

The *Declaration and Address* was in proof form when Alexander and the rest of the Campbell family arrived in America in the fall of 1809. Alexander, who had decided to become a minister, read the document, and nodded his enthusiastic approval. In fact, father and son discovered that independently they had reached similar positions. Alexander's convictions had taken shape during a year at the University of Glasgow where he had contact with movements interested in restoring primitive Christianity on a biblical basis. During his first few months in new surroundings, Alexander devoted himself to study in preparation for the ministry, and in the summer of 1810 began preaching.

While the scholarly Thomas remained influential among the "reformers," Alexander became the real leader. Between 1810 and the early 1830s, the movement adopted immersion as the mode of baptism; affiliated with Baptist associations; gained exposure through Alexander's sensational public debates and his periodical, *The Christian Baptist;* grew, thanks to the recruitment of several innovative evangelists; and finally broke with the Baptists. As the reformers and the Baptists were parting, Alexander replaced *The Christian Baptist* with *The Millennial Harbinger* in 1830. For more than thirty years, he used that paper to lead by letting readers know what he thought. He favored Disciples of Christ as a name, believed ministers should serve without salaries, advocated organized cooperation among congregations, and considered immersion the only scriptural mode of baptism while granting that there were unimmersed Christians. As the base for Alexander's travels, the center of his publishing enterprises and the site of the college he founded, the Campbell home at Bethany, West Virginia, for all practical purposes became the movement's headquarters.

Effective Evangelism

There naturally were other persons influential in Christian Church beginnings. Some were colorful enough to have novels written about them and a number made contributions no serious student of Disciples history would want to overlook. But since this chapter must be held to a brief summary, I will mention only two.

One is Walter Scott, who usually is listed as a founding father along with Stone and the Campbells. It was Scott—zealous, inventive, impulsive—who provided the Disciples an effective evangelism method. As evangelist of the Mahoning Baptist Association in eastern Ohio, he devised a "five-finger exercise" outlining the steps in conversion—faith, repentance, baptism, remission of sins, and gift of the Holy Spirit. In the fingers of one hand, Scott had a visual aid for teaching a lesson children could understand—and pass along to their parents. Baptist in name and immersionist practice only, he was far less interested in making new Baptists than in winning converts. While Baptists traditionally required a candidate for baptism to recount an emotional experience of salvation, Scott preached that it was enough for a person to confess belief and repent. He and the preachers who imitated him were highly successful. Long after their separation from the Baptists, the Disciples were using Scott's evangelism methods.

Then there was "Raccoon" John Smith of Kentucky. An unschooled but intelligent Baptist preacher, Smith became a reformer after meeting Alexander Campbell. He baptized so many converts that he earned the nickname "the Dipper," and spread the fire of reform so rapidly that former friends among the Baptists became his fierce enemies. Smith was in Kentucky what Scott was in Ohio, the evangelist who popularized the Disciples movement.

Christian-Disciple Union

The two groups—Christians and Disciples—inevitably discovered each other. They had much in common. They both were strong in the Kentucky-Ohio region. Yet there were differences between the movements. For one thing, the Christians had a higher regard for the clergy than Disciples did. Stone and Alexander Campbell exchanged sharp editorial jabs in their publications while the possibility of union was being discussed, and the two never became close friends. Their commitment to unity was too deep for them to stay apart, however.

Union of Christians and Disciples is dated from a meeting in Lexington, Kentucky, on New Year's Day 1832. "Raccoon" John Smith was chief spokesman for the Disciples and Stone represented the Christians. Their handshake, followed by the giving of the hand of fellowship among the rest of the participants, constituted approval. Since congregations of both streams were autonomous, actual union took several years. Smith from the Disciples side and John Rogers from the Christians were selected to ride together among the congregations completing the merger. An estimated 12,000 Disciples and 10,000 Christians came together in those early years of the 1830s.

Both names lived on. What was wanted was a New Testament name befitting a movement that would reunite the church. Alexander Campbell was sure "Disciples" or "Disciples of Christ" was ideal. He argued that it was descriptive, distinctive (no other group was using it) and ancient (followers of Jesus were known as disciples before they were called Christians). But Stone was equally satisfied with "Christians." He convinced Thomas Campbell and Walter Scott, but not Alexander. Detractors poked fun by applying the nicknames "Campbellites" and "Stoneites." That

17

dismayed the Disciples-Christians, who detested sectarian names. Still, they could not settle on one name or the other.

Rapid Expansion

In the thirty years leading up to the Civil War, the Disciples multiplied to more than 190,000 and expanded all the way to the Pacific Ocean. By 1900 the Christian Church had grown to approximately 1,120,000, in the United States. At the same time, the movement was developing in Canada, England, New Zealand, and Australia. In America, growth followed the frontier through the Midwest, across the Mississippi, into the Southwest and on westward. Settlers took with them what came to be called "the Plea"—Christian unity based on the New Testament. That approach made sense to frontier Americans, and the young movement that had not intended to become a separate church gained strength.

The greatest numerical strength of the Christian Church still lies in a crescent that starts in Kentucky; rises through Ohio, Indiana, and Illinois; crosses to Missouri and Kansas; and then swings south through Oklahoma and Texas. Approximately 58 percent of all American Disciples are in those eight states. California, Iowa, and North Carolina are the only other states that have more than 50,000.

Even before the Christian-Disciples union was consummated, congregations and individuals were cooperating to get essential work done. Smith and Rogers, sent out originally to promote the merger, soon were evangelizing together. Shortly, additional evangelists were being employed by county or district organizations. The first statewide assembly of Disciples was held in Indiana in 1839. Discussion of national organizations began around 1840 but the first, the American Christian Bible Society, was not formed until 1845. The first national convention was held in 1849 in Cincinnati, Ohio, and the main action of that gathering was creation of the American Christian Missionary Society for homeland as well as foreign missions. The next year, the society's first missionary, Dr. James T. Barclay, was sent to Jerusalem (he had persuaded the society that a New Testament people should begin there). Forerunners of most of our present organizations were at work by the turn of the century.

More colleges than could survive were started by the Disciples. Scott was the first president of Bacon College, which was founded at Georgetown, Kentucky, in 1836, and which eventually fed into what now is Transylvania University in Lexington. Alexander Campbell opened Bethany College in 1840 on a site carved from his West Virginia farm. Those were two of scores established to meet an obvious need for schools. I will list the other surviving educational institutions in a chapter on the Disciples' witness and service.

My home state, Oklahoma, was a microcosm of the booming brotherhood. There, a Territorial Missionary Society was organized in May 1891, only two years after the first Christian Church was planted. That first congregation had been started at Guthrie less than two weeks after the opening of the territory. E. F. Boggess, pastor at Guthrie and an agent of the Disciples' national Board of Church Extension, rode a Kentucky thoroughbred in the "Run" into the Cherokee Strip on September 16, 1893, to stake a claim for a church lot. Phillips University was founded at Enid in 1907, the year after Oklahoma became the forty-sixth of the United States. The frontier was closing and the Disciples' era of rapid expansion was ending.

Two Splits

Dissension that would escalate into two splits also began almost as soon as the Disciples and the Christians joined forces. Seeds of discord were in the movement's favorite slogans about restoration of New Testament Christianity. As George G. Beazley, Jr., put it in the interpretive book I already have mentioned, "Views of the founding fathers tended to crystallize into a rigid legalism, and this era [1866-1917 in Beazley's outline of history] was dominated by a Disciple scholasticism." One slogan was "Where the Scriptures speak, we speak; where the Scriptures are silent, we are silent." Another was "In essentials, unity; in nonessentials, liberty; in all things, charity." The rub came in deciding what the scriptural essentials were. Legalists contended that since they could find no specific mention of such things in the New Testament, the church should not have paid resident pastors, missionary societies, or musical instruments for use in worship. Over those issues, the present-day Churches of Christ began pulling away after the Civil War. They were counted separately in the 1906 census. Scholastics who stuck with the moderate body never were happy with directions the Disciples chose in the twentieth century. These "independents" gradually developed their own agencies, schools, publishing house, periodicals, conventions, and ministry. For many years, some "independent" and some "cooperative" ministers, congregations, and agencies pretended division was not occurring. A few of them truly thought of themselves as bridges. But sincere efforts at reconciliation failed. Finally in 1971 the third denomination from the Campbell-Stone movement was given a separate listing in the *Yearbook of American Churches* as the Christian Churches and Churches of Christ. Heritage is just about all the three groups have in common, and even that is variously interpreted.

Roles of Publications

Publications played important roles in both the remarkable growth of the Christian Church and its splintering. I already have mentioned Alexander Campbell's *The Millennial Harbinger* and Stone's *Christian Messenger.* But they were merely two of the most influential among numerous early papers. After the Civil War, the *Gospel Advocate,* edited in Nashville, Tennessee, by David Lipscomb, became the leading paper among the legalists, mainly southerners, who pulled away as the Churches of Christ. The two most important journals among moderates were *The Christian-Evangelist,* which could trace its history through editors to Stone, and the *Christian Standard,* which was begun in 1866. For many years, both of those publications spoke for the progressive majority. Persons who know the *Christian Standard* as the unofficial organ of the "independents" usually are surprised to learn that it originally was the leading advocate of cooperation. *The Christian-Evangelist* is an ancestor of *The Disciple,* which now is the journal of the Christian Church (Disciples of Christ).

Mainstream Maturation

In its second century, the mainstream of the Christian Church has matured in stages.

Within five years after their 1909 Centennial Convention in Pittsburgh, Pennsylvania, the Disciples had established a commission that later became the Council on Christian Unity (1910), chartered the Christian Board of Publication (1911), launched a Men and Millions Movement that enlisted more than 3,500 youth for Christian service and raised over $6 million for missions and colleges (1913), and formed what now is the Division of Higher Education (1914). With these and the missionary societies, benevolent association, ministerial relief board, and publications started in the last quarter of the nineteenth century, the Disciples had the basic outreach and service units a church needed.

Looking and beginning to act like a church, in 1907 the Disciples became charter members of the Federal Council of Churches, forerunner of the National Council of Churches (U.S.A.).

The next developmental stage—unification of organizations for greater efficiency—started in 1917 with the organization of the International Convention of Disciples of Christ. The next year, journals of several national agencies were combined in a new monthly magazine, *World Call* (merged into *The Disciple* in 1974). That move anticipated the formation of The United Christian Missionary Society in 1919 through a merger of six major agencies. Later, three of those organizations withdrew from the united society, but remained thoroughly cooperative. It was not until 1935 that Unified Promotion, predecessor of our present Church Finance Council, was created to raise and distribute funds for all Disciples causes, including state organizations and institutions. Slowly, almost hesitantly, after World War II, the International Convention developed a secretariat and assumed such brotherhoodwide functions as public relations and publication of the *Year Book and Directory*. A Council of Agencies, with no legislative or administrative power but much value for communication and coordination, was formed in 1952. Autonomous organizations were growing together.

Toward the end of that period, especially in the 1950s and 1960s, unification occurred at the state level. The old pattern differed from state to state, but the typical state had a convention, a missionary society for such purposes as starting congregations and helping pulpit committees find pastors, a Christian education board, a Christian Women's Fellowship, and a Christian Men's Fellowship. Now most states (current terminology is *regions*) have single organizations encompassing all functions and constituencies.

In the fifteen years after World War II, the Disciples rode the crest of church prosperity to success in two large cooperative efforts. The first was the Crusade for a Christian World (1947-1950) aimed at establishing new congregations, winning members, recruiting ministers and missionaries, and raising millions of dollars over and above regular offerings. Even though not all objectives were reached, the Crusade was experienced as a tremendous victory. On its heels came the Long Range Program of the 1950s, which involved annual program emphases and a goal of "Doubled Giving [for outreach causes] in the Decade." As it turned out, Disciples gave approximately 150 percent more for work financed through Unified Promotion in 1959-60 than they had in 1949-50. "This great achievement shames us for our little faith and gives hope and promise for the future," Wilbur H. Cramblet, chairman, told the Council of Agencies in 1960.

Churchly Wholeness

Before they dawned, the sixties had been aptly dubbed the "Decade of Decision." In a series of difficult decisions, the developmental phase we Disciples still are living through was started. The 1960 International Convention assembly authorized a representative Commission on Brotherhood Restructure to guide a churchwide process of organizational reform and renewal. Painstakingly, striving to be sensitive both to the Campbell-Stone heritage and to contemporary impulses toward change, the commission worked at its task. A report booklet prepared for a series of area assemblies of the International Convention in 1965 said that the aim of restructure was "to develop an organization that expresses the organic wholeness of the church." The Disciples, deliberately but not painlessly, were becoming a church. In 1968 the International Convention assembly adopted A Provisional Design for the Christian Church (Disciples of Christ), a quasi-constitutional document that described the church as a single body with interdependent "manifestations." Since I served as administrative secretary for the restructure commission, I know the freight every phrase in the design carries. I will describe the resulting structure more exactly in another chapter.

About the time the restructure commission was formed, the Disciples became participants in the Consultation on Church Union. That is a continuing effort by ten American denominations to form a united church. The consultation and other union conversations involving the Christian Church will be covered in a chapter on our unity ideal.

The 1960s were disturbing and exciting years. I look back with satisfaction on many of the things we Disciples did, frequently in cooperation with other churches. Launching our Reconciliation program to combat racism and poverty, for example. And continuing to relinquish to indigenous leadership control of overseas churches and institutions started by our missionaries. And integrating blacks and Hispanic Americans into regular church structures without wiping out their forums for self-expression. And dozens of other developments I will touch on later. I was also disappointed in certain aspects of the Disciples' performance in the sixties, particularly in the field of evangelism. The 1970 edition of the *Year Book and Directory of the Christian Church* reports almost 400,000 fewer members in the United States and Canada than the 1960 edition did.

Campaign for Attrition

Flagging zeal was not the main reason for the Christian Church's decline in membership, however. During the 1960s congregations reported more than 368,000 baptisms—just over 100 a day. There were at least half a million other additions, but transfers among Disciples congregations make the net gain impossible to calculate. Additions for the decade were not off enough to account for the large drop in membership.

The principal cause of our membership loss was a successful campaign by "independent" leaders to get congregations to withdraw their names from the official *Year Book and Directory* listing. In the last three years of the sixties, almost 3,000 congregations with a total membership estimated at more than 750,000 severed their ties with the Disciples. Admittedly, many of those congregations had been only marginally related to the church and needed very little urging to check out. Others, however, were participating congregations. They were spooked by letters warning falsely that restructure threatened congregations with loss of

23

freedoms, including the right to control their property. Of course, the Provisional Design carefully protected the integrity and rights of congregations, and no congregation has lost any measure of the right to govern its own affairs. The letter-writers even sent along withdrawal forms! Several congregations that withdrew have reversed their action and now are listed in the *Year Book and Directory*. While I was a regional minister in Texas, I visited some of the congregations that withdrew. Often leaders of those congregations would explain, "We were confused and misled by the mail we got. We didn't want to lose our property and figured it was better to be 'safe than sorry,' so we sent in the withdrawal form."

A. Dale Fiers was coping with that fabricated internal crisis as well as the substantive crises wracking America when the Provisional Design was adopted, and he became the church's first general minister and president. No one more nearly personifies the Disciples dream than Dr. Fiers does. A pastor for more than twenty years, he was named president of The United Christian Missionary Society in 1951, then in 1964 succeeded Gaines M. Cook as executive secretary of the International Convention. It has been said of Dr. Fiers that no other person helped shape the Disciples more profoundly since Alexander Campbell. I remember that when he spoke to the 1960 International Convention assembly on "One God, One World, One Mission," he articulated the dream that became reality during the next decade through restructure: "The oneness of our mission calls for a churchly relationship between congregations at the various levels of brotherhood life, and in all the areas of intercongregational fellowship and cooperation." Though he has been widely recognized as an able administrator and Christian statesman, Dr. Fiers is most appreciated for his embodiment of the early Disciples' passion to proclaim the saving gospel of Jesus Christ and to bring about the unity of the church.

Scriptures

When I was a regional minister, members of pulpit committees often would tell me emphatically, "We want a Bible preacher!" As heads around the room nodded agreement, I would wonder uneasily what was meant by Bible preacher: One who straightforwardly would confront the people with the radical demands of the gospel? One who would advocate the Christian life as it is portrayed in the New Testament? One who would teach the people to study the Scriptures expectantly, hoping to find something new and valuable? One who would drive home every sermonic point with a cleverly chosen proof text? One who would tell lots of Bible stories but never really relate them to contemporary issues? Or what?

We Disciples of Christ always have called ourselves a Bible people. Or as some prefer to phrase it, a New Testament people. Slogans handed down from founders of the Christian Church reflect that self-image: "Bible names for Bible things," "No creed but Christ" and "Where the Scriptures speak, we speak." In what sense is it true today that we Disciples are a Bible people?

Founders' Discoveries

The acknowledged founding fathers—Barton W. Stone, Thomas and Alexander Campbell, and Walter Scott—approached the Bible in the spirit of excited discovery. From their separate experiences with rigidly divided Christianity, the four turned to the New Testament individually, and found freedom and unity.

In his examination prior to ordination as a Presbyterian minister in 1798, Stone said that he accepted the Westminster

25

Confession "as far as I see it consistent with the word of God." His bent already showed. Five years later, as the Synod of Kentucky discussed charges of unorthodoxy against two of them, five "revival men," including Stone, renounced the authority of the synod. They declared their right to appeal from the Presbyterian creed to the Bible. Stone helped form a maverick presbytery, but in less than a year signed *The Last Will and Testament of the Springfield Presbytery.* That document willed, among other things, "that the people henceforth take the Bible as the only sure guide to heaven."

Thomas Campbell, horrified by division among Christians, concluded that the way to restore unity was to abandon the denominations' competing systems of theology and return to what they all had in common, the New Testament. Having withdrawn from the presbytery and synod of his branch of the Presbyterian church, Campbell formed the Christian Association of Washington, Pennsylvania, and in 1809 wrote a *Declaration and Address* setting forth the association's views. The central idea was that Christians could "restore unity, peace and purity to the whole church of God" by "rejecting human opinions and the inventions of men" and "taking the divine word alone for our rule." The New Testament was seen as a perfect "constitution for the worship, discipline, and government" of the church and a "rule for the particular duties of its members." Ironically, the elder Campbell's words about the sufficiency of the New Testament as a constitution have been quoted in justifying two splits from the Christian Church. But ground for reunion, not separation, is what he saw in the Scriptures.

With iconoclastic fervor, Thomas Campbell's son, Alexander, described and expounded the church he found in the New Testament. He used his first periodical, *The Christian Baptist,* to promote what he termed "restoration of the ancient order of things." His later journal, *The Millennial Harbinger,* was less radical in that it admitted the value of some expedients not expressly called for in the New Testament—missionary societies and colleges, for example. In *The Christian System,* first published in 1835 and used as the standard Disciples textbook for generations, Campbell presented an orderly statement of what he believed the New Testament taught. Critics charged that he had produced a creed, but Campbell staunchly denied it. Neither *The*

Christian System nor views of "any fallible mortal" should take the place of the Bible as "the foundation of all Christian union and communion," the Disciples' most influential founder insisted. Walter Scott's study of the Scriptures yielded the "gospel restored." That was his term for a plan of salvation he traced from the New Testament, particularly the Acts of the Apostles. Scott held that apostolic preaching for conversation was presenting the "truth to the believed" and "evidences necessary to warrant belief." Faith, then, was a person's intelligent response to information recorded in the New Testament and re-presented convincingly. Scott saw in the Bible not only "the great fact to be believed . . . that he [Jesus] is the Son of God" but also a plan for securing a faith response.

In light of the movement's New Testament orientation, it is not surprising that the Disciples' first national organization was the American Christian Bible Society, formed in 1845.

Heavy emphasis on the Bible in schools started by the Disciples also was predictable. Alexander Campbell claimed that Bethany College, which he chartered in 1840, was "the only College known to us in the civilized world founded upon the Bible." Suspicion of theology was one accompaniment of restorationism, so until recently the Christian Church's graduate schools for ministerial education tended to have "college of the Bible" or "school of religion" in their names rather than "theological seminary" or "divinity school." The seminaries I attended at Phillips University and Texas Christian University, for example, were at that time named College of the Bible and Brite College of the Bible, respectively (now The Graduate Seminary and Brite Divinity School).

Canonized Opinions

What the founding fathers did not fully recognize is that it is impossible for anyone to interpret the Bible without expressing human opinions. One person's private opinion is another person's divine word. There is no such thing as a pure exposition of what the New Testament says.

Alexander Campbell's believing sincerely that *The Christian System* presented only revealed truth did not make it so. But before that venerated leader was dead, his opinions were being used as tests of fellowship. Legalists in the movement did not seem to notice that Campbell's views changed on some of the very issues that became divisive—recognition of unimmersed church members as Christians, for example, and missionary societies. Strangely, the scholastics failed to see that a particular pattern of New Testament "restoration" had become a standard of orthodoxy. Although Campbell was not known for his humility, canonization of his interpretation of the Scriptures would have shocked him. He doubtless would have been even more appalled to find that another person's interpretation had become as authoritative as the Bible itself.

The New Testament is not as simple as the founders and some of their spiritual descendants supposed. It was produced by a young church that existed in a variety of forms in widely differing communities. The documents that became part of the canon were written to meet diverse needs of that time. Youngest of the New Testament books was written around A.D. 150, long before the church encountered the institutional problems for which nineteenth-century restorationists would seek divinely revealed solutions. The only way to get unambiguous answers to some questions from the New Testament is to select the scriptures very carefully.

If the restorationists had not canonized opinions, they could not have coped with some of the issues their legalism generated. Should the church use organs and other musical instruments in worship? The New Testament gives no answer. Mainstream Disciples concluded that the Scriptures' silence meant that use of organs was no big deal. But the conservative wing that became the Churches of Christ decided that the New Testament's silence was tantamount to a command not to use organs. As a result, around the end of the nineteenth century, an opinion deduced from what the Scriptures did not say about musical instruments helped divide the movement.

Another opinion some Disciples have used almost like a creed is that every word of the Bible must be taken as literally true, scientifically as well as religiously. To adopt such a position is to degrade the Scriptures. The Bible is a book of religious truth—for Christians, the authoritative book. It is not a book of science, or even a book of secular history. Its value for Christians is not diminished by what humans have learned since the canon was closed. As William R. Baird, Jr., writing for the Disciples' *Panel*

28

of Scholars Reports (Vol. II, *The Reconstruction of Theology.* Bethany Press, 1963), expressed it, "The Bible, particularly the New Testament, gains its authority as witness to the revelation of God in Jesus Christ." Such an affirmation claims more for the Bible, cover to cover, than crude literalism does.

That probably is enough about what I consider to be misuse of the Scriptures.

Intelligent Approach to the Bible

Disciples characteristically believe that the Bible is understandable. Not uniformly easy to understand, but intelligible. Not just to professional ministers and theologians, but to lay members of the church.

Inquiring, open minds are needed to get the full intended meanings from books of the Old and New Testaments. Devoted study as well as devotional reading are required for real comprehension. Knowing that the Bible should be approached intelligently, Alexander Campbell offered rules for interpreting the Scriptures in *The Christian System.* "On opening any book in the sacred Scriptures," his first rule advised, "consider first the historical circumstances of the book. These are the order, the title, the date, the place and the occasion of it." Not entirely original but clearly ahead of his time, Campbell said biblical passages "are to be translated, interpreted and understood according to the same code of laws and principles of interpretation by which other ancient writings are translated and understood." Controversies raged deep into the twentieth century as scholars labeled "liberals" used principles of study similar to those proposed by Campbell. In the Christian Church, a lengthy battle between critical scholarship and biblical literalism was waged in columns of *The Christian-Evangelist* and the *Christian Standard,* which still leans toward fundamentalism as the unofficial journal of the "independents." That fight is behind us. Nowadays, most Disciples welcome whatever light our best minds can shed on the church's most important book.

In 1956, convinced that "the time was ripe for Disciples to reexamine their beliefs and doctrines in a scholarly way," two units of the church, The United Christian Missionary Society and the Board of Higher Education, formed a fifteen-member Panel of Scholars for that purpose. W. B. Blakemore, chairman, observed in his foreword to the panel's three-volume collection of papers (*The Panel of Scholars Reports*), that the group never thought of itself as "an official committee . . . commissioned to write a new theology" for the Disciples. Rather, the panel was asked to "search out and clarify the theological, biblical, sociological and historical issues" Disciples might profitably talk about. Speaking for the sponsoring agencies, W. M. Wickizer explained, "The tenets held by our fathers in the faith needed to be restudied and validated or modified in the light of modern scholarship." The panel's published reports have no standing as official positions of the Christian Church on the topics dealt with. Nevertheless, the panel rendered a significant unofficial service to the Disciples in helping us rethink and update our rich Bible-based tradition. That work by some of our ablest scholars was one constructive step in a process of reformation (call it renewal if you prefer, or even restoration if you can strip that word of its legalism) that I hope will never end. Good scholarship can only open the Scriptures wider for us.

From their beginnings, though, Disciples have sensed the importance of having Bible students in the pews as well as in the pulpits and in the universities. Frankly, there is far too little intelligent searching of the Scriptures by lay people. Yet, about the time I am ready to conclude that members of the Christian Church no longer use their Bibles, I encounter a lay person who not only has been reading scriptures but also has been delving into related contemporary literature. About the time the Panel of Scholars was beginning its work, M. Jack Suggs wrote a book to help lay people read the Bible with greater understanding (*The Layman Reads His Bible.* Bethany Press, 1957). It is a small book—a fast reader could get through it in one evening—but it is extremely helpful. Suggs explains why readers should be aware of such factors as the lands in which the Bible was written, the history of the Old and New Testament periods, and the original languages—Hebrew, Aramaic, and Greek. Even though as a New Testament scholar he uses more sophisticated techniques, Suggs commends use of Alexander Campbell's W-Key—opening the Scriptures by asking "who, when, where, to whom, and why?" Other nontechnical books on how to read the Bible profitably are available. I wish that every Disciple who has been putting off private study of the Scriptures would get started.

It is easier now than it was when my generation was young. Since then, new translations and paraphrases have been published in modern English. Many of us remember the bitter opposition to the Revised Standard Version authorized by the National Council of Churches (U.S.A.) and published just after World War II. There even were charges that some changes in the English text had been made by Communist atheists. That controversy seems strange and remote now—thank goodness! The newer *Good News for Modern Man, The New Testament in Today's English Version,* published by the American Bible Society, was received enthusiastically. It has been released in colorful editions that do not look much like our black leatherbound Bibles, and it has sold on newsstands with other paperbacks. More remarkable has been the popular acceptance of Kenneth Taylor's *Living Bible,* which he candidly admits is a paraphrase "from a rigid evangelical position" rather than a new translation. Modern translators have had use of original language manuscripts much older than those available to scholars who worked on the King James Version. They also have known more about the conditions under which various books were written. Consequently, English used in some of the new versions comes much closer to communicating the authors' meanings. My own personal preference is *The New English Bible.* It is written in easy-to-read contemporary language, but is still a faithful translation and not just a paraphrase. A very useful procedure in Bible study today is to read a passage in three or four versions, letting each bring out facets of meaning.

There is no way to overstate the importance through the years of the Sunday church school and other Christian education in local Disciples congregations. I was fortunate to be reared in a congregation (First Christian Church, Cushing, Oklahoma) that placed a premium on quality Christian education. As I recall, there always was an abundance of first-class literature. More important, however, was the care taken in the selection of church school teachers like Mrs. Grace Testerman, Mrs. E. O. Derrick, and Mrs. Sam Tennis. It is no accident that after nearly fifty years these three women are vivid in my memory. They were ardent students of the Bible who seemed able not so much to communicate ancient history, but contemporary reality—especially in the quality of their own lives. Besides the regular Sunday church school, many congregations now offer through-the-week classes, weekend retreats, guidance for family study in the home and other educational opportunities. Regrettably we Disciples have our share of congregations that provide almost nothing educational.

Authority in the Church

The Bible has a unique role in the church. It is the point of reference for all that happens—worship, proclamation, study, group action, individual service—everything. Still, the book itself is not worshiped. That would be bibliolatry. The Bible is authoritative because it witnesses to the revelation of God in Jesus Christ. It is a one-of-a-kind record of what God did and how people responded. It is not the Word. But it is an inspired and inspiring witness to the Word, who is a living person, Christ. For that reason, the Bible has a place of authority in the church which no other book, however great, could have.

As witness to the revelation of God in Christ, the Bible is timeless. Its message will be as pertinent to my grandchildren as it was to the church that established the New Testament canon. The Scriptures were equally relevant to Europe's sixteenth-century Reformation and to America's twentieth-century crisis in race relations. The New Testament spoke to Africans who heard its words first from white missionaries and still witnesses to Zairians who read for themselves.

Nor is the Bible limited by space or events or politics. Sharp in my memory are the exchange visits between American and Russian church leaders in 1974 and 1975. Those of us who participated were conscious of the differences between the social systems in which our churches exist. At the same time, we were keenly aware of the New Testament-based faith that makes us one in Christ.

We who call ourselves Disciples still are a Bible people. True, most of us are less confident than our ancestors that we follow the New Testament more closely than other Christians. As our forefathers did, though, we recognize the unique authority of the Scriptures as witness to the revelation of God in Christ, and the measuring stick for what we believe and do.

Unity Ideal

The ideal of Christian unity is to Disciples of Christ what basketball is to Indiana, hospitality is to the South, and nonviolence is to Quakers. It is part of our identity. It is our middle name. It is "the Plea"—the distinctive cause that has been the Christian Church's reason for existing. About midpoint in the twentieth century, soon after formation of the World Council of Churches and the National Council of Churches (U.S.A.), Howard E. Short wrote a little study book on Disciples in the ecumenical movement and titled it *Christian Unity Is Our Business*. And right up to the present, we Disciples who have been steeped in our heritage feel especially called to work for unity.

Founders' Objective

In the chapter on Disciples origins, I pointed out that the founding fathers thought they were launching a movement to unite Christians, not starting another denomination. Then, in the chapter on the Scriptures, I dealt with the movement's strategy— to find common ground in a restoration of the New Testament church. What I intend to do in this chapter is reflect on whether, and in what ways, the Christian Church still is pressing toward the original objective.

Thomas Campbell's *Declaration and Address* and the Stone-signed *Last Will and Testament of the Springfield Presbytery,* the two earliest important documents of Disciples history, also are remarkably nonsectarian statements of the ideal of Christian unity. The first point of each document asserts that the unity of the church is a given fact that denominationalism cannot negate.

33

Campbell's treatise affirms that the "church of Christ upon earth is essentially, intentionally, and constitutionally one"; and the will that dissolved Stone's presbytery says that "there is but one Body, and one Spirit, even as we are called in one hope of our calling." The *Declaration and Address* terms division "a horrid evil . . . antichristian . . . antiscriptural . . . antinatural," and an obstacle to evangelism. The movement that became a brotherhood and eventually a church sought to make visible and effective the natural unity of the body of Christ.

From our vantage point in the last quarter of the twentieth century, we can see the founders' naiveté. For one thing, they underestimated the persistence of denominations: the named, institutionalized divisions among Christians would not die quickly. The Campbells, Stone, Walter Scott, and the others also misjudged the difficulty of achieving unity by returning to the New Testament essentials: most, if not all, churches would claim that base. Too, the Disciples fathers romanticized what they were doing: they could not see themselves as many of their contemporaries did—patriarchs of a new denomination. Understand, none of my Monday-morning quarterbacking detracts from the rightness of the objectives those idealists had—and passed on to us.

Inevitably, some parts of the Campbell-Stone movement adopted a "come join us" stance. The strictest restorationists felt that the movement was beyond and superior to the denominations. They were certain that they had found the simple New Testament faith and undefiled church practice on which Christians could unite. All that was needed to achieve unity was for people to leave the denominations and become "Christians only." This messianic strain has continued in the Churches of Christ, the group that separated around the beginning of this century, and to a lesser degree in the "independent" Christian Churches. Explaining lucidly what he called "restoration legalism," David Edwin Harrell, Jr., a Church of Christ educator, said in a Disciples of Christ Historical Society lecture, "From my theological point of view, the group to which I belong is the church universal. . . . Members of the Churches of Christ did not invent the idea of being God's 'peculiar people,' but they are surely some of the staunchest advocates of the concept."[3]

3. *Disciples and the Church Universal,* Reed Lectures for 1966. Disciples of Christ Historical Society, 1967.

Mutuality in the Quest

Mainstream Disciples chose a different style. It is the style of the ecumenical movement. *Mutuality* and *reciprocity* are words Ronald E. Osborn, one of the Disciples' most insightful historians, has used to describe it. His lecture in the same series in which Professor Harrell spoke was entitled "Witness and Receptivity" (more colloquially, we might say give and take). Osborn showed that mutuality, the giving and receiving of gifts from God, is an apostolic principle, then told how it works in the ecumenical movement and church union. He observed that it "finds expression in movements toward a church . . . which incorporates into its *common* life the gifts which believers have previously held in their separate traditions, a church where all disciples will have opportunity both to witness and to receive for mutual strengthening."

The capacity of the Disciples to give and take has enriched my own life and ministry. Neither too rigidly structured nor liturgically bound nor dogmatic, Disciples are able to borrow rather easily from other traditions. Sometimes the result is something of a hodgepodge. More often, the willingness to receive as well as witness facilitates a happier exchange of God's gifts.

I experienced reciprocity in the 1974-75 exchange visits by representatives of churches in the United States and the Soviet Union. My visit to Russian churches opened up for me a new appreciation for the way Orthodox churches use worship and art to communicate the Christian faith. Largely restricted to the church building itself for education and evangelism, the Russian Orthodox Church has been able to transmit the gospel through the drama and pageantry of its centuries-old divine liturgy. I could not help but be impressed. On the other hand, Bishop Makary of Uman, when he presented me with a jeweled fleury cross for the Christian Church, said that he admired the Disciples' simplicity and their obvious love for one another.

We Disciples have much to offer, not the least of which is the kind of freedom that permits varieties of opinions and practices in one church. A long time ago, we recognized that other churches share our hope for Christian unity and that they have equally cherished contributions to make. We call the common quest the ecumenical movement.

Ecumenical Century

It was about the time the Christian Church turned 100 that the ecumenical movement was born and the Disciples' interest in unity was renewed. During the previous forty years, the Disciples had participated in several notable efforts that crossed denominational lines. One was the Sunday school movement, which in 1872 began issuing the Uniform Lessons used by many denominations. Another was the Young People's Society of Christian Endeavor, founded in 1881. Toward the end of the nineteenth century, there was widespread discussion of proposals for a federation in which American churches could retain their separate identities, but work together. But serious interdenominational planning for such an organization did not begin until the first decade of the twentieth century.

When the Federal Council of Churches of Christ in America, an ancestor of the present National Council of Churches, was constituted in 1908, a Disciples delegation was present. Federation had been a controversial topic in Christian Church conventions and publications for years. Opponents warned that the proposed organization would "recognize the denominations"; that in joining, the Disciples would accept denominational status; and that federation could become a permanent substitute for real union. The majority, however, felt that the Disciples should belong. It was generally conceded that the Christian Church had no governing body to settle the issue *officially*. So a public meeting on the single topic of Disciples membership in the federation was held outside regular sessions of the 1907 General Convention, and participation was heartily approved.

That set the pattern. Since then, the Disciples have been vigorous participants in interdenominational organizations at world, national, regional, state, and local levels.

Theme for the Christian Church's great centennial convention in 1909 was "The union of all believers, on a basis of Holy Scripture, to the end that the world may be evangelized." It was appropriate both for a celebration of the 100th anniversary of the *Declaration and Address* and for the kickoff of an ecumenical century.

The next year, Peter Ainslie III, president of the Disciples' General Convention, called for a recommitment to the cause of

Christian unity. Specifically, he proposed creation of a special organization to promote Disciples interest and participation in efforts toward union. His suggestion was accepted and the Disciples formed the Council on Christian Union (now the Council on Christian Unity). No other church had such a thing. Ainslie, pastor of Christian Temple in Baltimore, served as president of the council until 1925 and personally led the Disciples into some of their ecumenical relationships.

The first peg on which the modern ecumenical movement hangs also was driven in 1910. That was the holding of a world missionary conference in Edinburgh. The other large pegs are the Universal Christian Conference on Life and Work in Stockholm in 1925 and the First World Conference on Faith and Order in Lausanne in 1927. From those three conferences stretch the main strands that have been woven into the World Council of Churches.

It is easy to understand why Paul A. Crow, Jr., president of our Council on Christian Unity since mid-1974, says 1910 "is accepted as the symbolic moment when the will toward unity was reborn in the twentieth century among the churches."[4]

In 1908 Charles Clayton Morrison, who represented the Disciples in many ecumenical meetings, bought a struggling Christian Church paper inclined toward liberalism and interdenominational interests. That periodical, *The Christian Century*, became thoroughly ecumenical and earned international acclaim as an independent chronicler and critic of the church.

Interdenominational Organizations

In the 1980s, we Disciples are deeply involved in a variety of interdenominational organizations. We help shape their policies. We use their programs as our own. We provide staff members and volunteers. We cultivate relationships that bear fruit later apart from the organizations. We act as Christians united in situations where we would be ineffective speaking or working separately.

---

4. Crow has provided an excellent commentary on "The Christian Church (Disciples of Christ) in the Ecumenical Movement" in the book edited by George G. Beazley, Jr., *The Christian Church (Disciples of Christ): An Interpretative Examination in the Cultural Context.* Bethany Press, 1973.

The organization about which American Disciples have heard most is the National Council of Churches. It does not follow, however, that members of the Christian Church are well informed about the NCC. It is woefully misunderstood. In years of interpreting and defending the council, I have found that most people have read or heard that its boards make statements on controversial issues. Relatively few people are familiar with the NCC's programs. Church World Service, for example, which has helped resettle more than 300,000 refugees and has provided over five billion pounds of relief supplies on every continent. Or the Friendship Press, which publishes outreach education materials used by many denominations. Or the communication commission through which the cooperating churches do network radio and television programming. Or the stewardship commission, which does research and prepares materials beneficial to local congregations. Or joint curriculum development for the mentally retarded, the deaf and the emotionally disturbed. In all, there are more than 70 specific areas in which the 32 member churches work together in the NCC. The more you know about the National Council, the more you appreciate it.

I am one of the Disciples on the 350-member governing board of the NCC. Same as the delegations of the other churches, ours is representative of the laity, youth, and minorities as well as the church's professional leaders.

With more than 300 churches in 100 countries as members, the World Council of Churches comes closer than any other single organization to living up to the adjective *ecumenical*. (A few years ago, I had to define *ecumenical* every time I wrote or spoke it, but nowadays just about everyone uses it when referring to the whole household of Christian faith.) The WCC has working relationships with additional churches that have not sought membership—the Roman Catholic Church, for example, and the Seventh-day Adventists. Since the council's constituting assembly in 1948, Disciples delegations have been on hand. But the WCC is more than an assembly held every seven years. The council is an essential instrument for certain Disciples units that have international responsibilities—our Division of Overseas Ministries, for instance, and the Council on Christian Unity. Titles of some of the departments and working sections indicate the breadth of the council's program: faith and order; world mission and evangelism; interchurch aid, refugee and world service; racial justice; dialogue with people of living faiths and ideologies; education. As I write this, I am preparing for participation in the World Council's sixth (1983) assembly in Vancouver, British Columbia, hopeful that the churches will be drawn even closer together as their representatives discuss the theme, "Jesus Christ: The Life of the World."

No doubt, the type of interdenominational organization in which the most Disciples are involved is the regional, state, county, or city council of churches. Nowadays, more and more of those units are being called conferences or ecumenical councils, which often signifies that they include the Roman Catholic Church or others that until recently were not joiners. Some local and regional federations are many years old, but the bulk of them have been created since World War II. The *Yearbook of American and Canadian Churches,* the most comprehensive storehouse of facts on the churches, admits that its list is incomplete, adding, "If a composite list of all local and regional ecumenical instrumentalities were compiled, it would number into many thousands." That large count would include not only the broad-spectrum councils concerned with all major church interests but also such special-purpose units as telephone counseling services, mass media communication centers, and poverty programs. Since it is their nature to be cooperative and to seek Christian unity, Disciples have helped form, direct, and staff many of these organizations.

Shortly before I went to Texas in 1969 as the Disciples' regional minister, the Christian Church had participated in the formation of the Texas Conference of Churches. At the time, it was unique—with a membership that ranged from Roman Catholics to Friends, the most inclusive ecumenical agency anywhere. Roy J. Cates and James C. Suggs, both Disciples, were the first two executive directors of the conference. In my years of involvement, I marveled at the scope of what the churches were doing together—discussing heavy theological issues in an annual faith and order conference, ministering to Mexican-American farmworkers in the Rio Grande Valley, training key leaders in twice-a-year laboratory schools, seeking funds to support community self-development programs and so on. I am certain that Disciples participation in organizations like the Texas Conference is in keeping with the idealistic objective of the founders of our church.

In the past quarter of a century, the ecumenical spirit has produced a variety of useful organizations centered around particular needs or opportunities. I could not list all of them, much less tell what each has meant to the Disciples. But to indicate the strength and diversity of church cooperation, I will give a few examples. There is United Ministries in Higher Education, the agency through which ten denominations minister to more than 1,100 campuses. And Religion in American Life, the agency that secures millions of dollars worth of mass media advertising free for the churches and synagogues. And Church Women United, which brings women across denominational lines to study, worship, serve, and build bridges of understanding. And the Career Development Council, which is establishing a network of accredited career counseling centers for professional church workers. There are many others.

Approximately 100 Disciples belong to a fellowship known as Disciples of Christ in Ecumenical Ministry. That membership roster is not a complete list of Disciples in such staff positions, however.

Some Disciples usually are in the forefront of nearly any worthwhile cooperative venture. I observed this most meaningfully during the Little Rock racial crisis of the late 1950s. Not only were courageous local pastors like Colbert Cartwright at the center of efforts to secure equal rights for all citizens, but regional Disciples leadership engaged in the establishment of a Little Rock Conference on Religion and Race to which many ascribe credit for the high degree of racial reconciliation that has occurred in the city since then. Similarly in other communities, Disciples have provided part of the impetus for the day-care center, the cooperative church school for exceptional children, the interdenominational Holy Week services, the jail ministry, and the crisis intervention service. We would have to change our identities to not cooperate.

No amount of interdenominational cooperation is the same as the uniting of churches. Not even the quality of commitment found in an organization like United Ministries in Higher Education. Actual union is a different thing, and is closer to the ideal we Disciples still have.

Church Union Conversations

Since the union of the Disciples and the Christians in 1832 (I covered that in the chapter on origins), the Christian Church (Disciples of Christ) has not united with any group in either the United States or Canada. There have been sincere negotiations, but no unions; courtships, but no marriages. Conversations still alive could yet produce the first North American union involving Disciples.

The group with which the Christian Church has had the greatest number of talks about union over the longest period of time is the American Baptist Churches (formerly Northern Baptist Convention). A string of frustrated overtures and conversations runs from 1841 to 1952. A lingering benefit from the last effort is some joint publishing, one example of which is the *Hymnbook for Christian Worship* released in 1970 by the Bethany Press (Disciples) and the Judson Press (Baptist).

Conversations with the Congregational Christian Church started long before that body united with the Evangelical and Reformed Church in 1957 to form the United Church of Christ. Almost before that union was completed in 1961, the Disciples and UCC began union talks. Commissions representing the two churches had five sessions before deciding in the mid-sixties to suspend their conversations to give undivided attention to the more inclusive Consultation on Church Union.

By 1979 both churches agreed that those talks should be resumed. The St. Louis General Assembly adopted a resolution establishing a covenant with the United Church of Christ for a six-year period to "work together toward embodying God's gift of oneness in Jesus Christ." During those six years (1979-1985), three broad tasks of Christian witness and theological reflection were identified for work and study across the life of both churches: (1) the theology and practice of Baptism and the Lord's Supper; (2) the nature, task and equipping of ministry, both ordained and lay; and (3) appropriate forms of mission today. A joint steering committee of ten persons from each church was appointed to give leadership and direction to this new venture. The bilateral conversations are being conducted within the broader framework of the Consultation on Church Union.

It was the United Church of Christ, with which the Disciples already were in conversation, that asked in 1962 that the Christian Church be invited to participate in the Consultation on Church Union. A Disciples delegation attended the second plenary of the consultation in 1963 and we have been involved ever since. From the original four churches Eugene Carson Blake challenged to seek a united church "truly catholic, truly evangelical, and truly reformed," the list of full participants has grown to ten—African Methodist Episcopal, African Methodist Episcopal Zion, Christian Methodist Episcopal, Christian Church (Disciples of Christ), Episcopal Church, National Council of Community Churches, Presbyterian Church in the U.S., United Church of Christ, United Methodist Church and United Presbyterian Church in the U.S.A. Delegates to the 1965 Lexington, Kentucky, plenary of the consultation worshiped and celebrated the Lord's Supper in the nearby Cane Ridge Meeting House (why Disciples consider that old log building where Barton W. Stone preached a shrine to Christian unity is evident). Paul A. Crow, Jr., now president of the Disciples' Council on Christian Unity, became the consultation's first general secretary in 1968 and served until 1974. George G. Beazley, Jr., who at the time of his death in 1973 was president of the Council on Christian Unity, was chairman of the consultation for the first biennium of the seventies.

In 1970 the consultation released for study and response *A Plan of Union for the Church of Christ Uniting*. Responses of the churches showed substantial agreement with chapters of the plan dealing with theological matters, but dissatisfaction with sections on structure of the proposed Church of Christ Uniting. In light of that, the 1973 plenary decided to move ahead with revision of portions of the plan that might serve as a theological basis, but approach the problem of design or polity differently.

The new strategy was to discover the kinds of structures that develop naturally as congregations of the participating churches live and work together in "generating communities." It was a bottom-up as opposed to top-down process of design. The intent was for each generating community to include at least one congregation of each Consultation on Church Union church in the community. A generating community covenants with the consultation to try to function as a united parish, and to share its experiences and insights.

The 15th plenary session of the Consultation on Church Union was held in March 1982, in Louisville, Kentucky, almost exactly twenty years after COCU was constituted in early 1962. The 1982 plenary represented a kind of watershed in the life of the Consultation. It affirmed a process of covenanting as the appropriate way ahead for the Consultation in the quest for visible unity in a church truly catholic, truly evangelical, and truly reformed. The plenary instructed the church order commission to prepare proposals for covenanting that include the following elements: mutual recognizing of the churches; claiming the emerging theological consensus; recognizing/reconciling their ministries; initiating regular eucharistic fellowship; exercising social and personal mission, including common mission in such areas as justice, peace, and liberation; and commissioning "apostolic collegia" (councils of oversight).

The last mentioned element is a new idea, and generated a great deal of interest. Such groups, at national, regional and local levels, composed of leaders from each church, would have the responsibility of overseeing the convenanting process in a variety of ways—joint ordinations, confirmations, and common mission, to name only three.

Since 1969 Canadian Disciples have been engaged in union conversations with the United Church of Canada. "Principles of Church Union" are being developed that seek to ensure continuing integrity for both churches.

Unity on the Growing Edges

As it was in the frontier situation faced by the Campbells, Stone, and Scott, Christian unity is seen as a powerful ally in present-day settings where the church struggles against odds. Necessity is combining forces with recognition of the sin of division to bring Christians together on the growing edges of the church. It has been happening overseas for a good many years now, and it is beginning to occur in the Disciples' homeland.

In 1955, as the younger churches around the world were speaking out for unity, the world division of The United Christian Missionary Society (now the Division of Overseas Ministries) began implementing *A Strategy of World Mission*. In brief, that document said that henceforth Disciples in the United States and

Canada gradually would turn control of missionary-planted churches around the world over to indigenous leaders. With self-determination would go the right to decide to participate in the formation of united churches. (I'll come back to this in a chapter on our structures for witness and service to humanity.) For the next quarter-century the Disciples have been working with strong union churches in Latin America, Asia, and Africa. Although the Christian Church in North America started missionary work in only a dozen countries, it now is involved in partnership with churches in nearly half the countries of the world. The 1981 Anaheim General Assembly adopted an overall operating philosophy for overseas mission, affirming the ecumenical approach, partnership as opposed to paternalism, and emphasis on the poor and oppressed.[5]

In Zaire, the united church is headed by Itofe Bokambanza Bokeleale, an African who previously held the top office in the Disciples community in that country. When Canon Burgess Carr, then executive secretary of the All-Africa Conference of Churches, visited Disciples offices in Indianapolis early in 1975 and talked about his participation in the upcoming San Antonio General Assembly of the Christian Church, he commented about the strong ecumenical emphasis on the program. He said it was typical of Disciples involvement with the churches in Africa, and he assumed in the rest of the world, where emphasis is on an ecumenical witness. "It is easy for one to see how persons like Itofe Bokambanza Bokeleale come to leadership in places like Zaire." Bokeleale is a member of the central committee of the World Council of Churches.

Back home, Disciples are participating in ecumenical planning for congregations in new towns, the major communities springing up in what was open country. In some regions, the Christian Church does all new church development in concert with other denominations.

One of my Texas Methodist friends said to me: "You Disciples help keep my hopes for Christian unity alive. You haven't really united with anyone in your whole history, yet you keep insisting the church is one. You never seem to become disillusioned about

5. Copies of *General Principles and Policies, Division of Overseas Ministries,* are available from Division of Overseas Ministries, P.O. Box 1986, Indianapolis, IN 46206.

the possibilities for church union." We who call ourselves Disciples must not forget that by our attitudes and actions we influence the will of other Christians to reach toward the ideal of unity.

Our confusing double name is peculiarly appropriate for a church that was born with a wish to "die, be dissolved, and sink into union with the Body of Christ at large."[6] The generic first part, *Christian Church,* points to our objective of unity. The distinguishing second part, *Disciples of Christ,* reminds us that we have not arrived.

---

6. *The Last Will and Testament of the Springfield Presbytery.*

——————— Diversity ———————

Suppose computer-aided research were used in an effort to categorize the Christian Church (Disciples of Christ). Imagine it. One of the independent research organizations sends interviewers to ask a sampling of Disciples a battery of questions. The aim is to find out what labels the Christian Church should be given—conservative or liberal, pietist or activist, unitarian or trinitarian, and so on. Answers collected by the interviewers are key-encoded on a magnetic tape. Then a computer searches the tape, sorts the responses and prints the Disciples' labels—one for every category. Perhaps that fantasy is overdrawn. But it is a fact that the Disciples are not easily classified.

We Disciples consider our diversity almost as valuable as what we have in common. In fact, we say that we want "unity, not uniformity," or "unity with diversity." Our biblical names, *Christian Church* and *Disciples of Christ,* are intentionally inclusive. We do not think Christians have to be unanimous in thought and action to be in the same church.

Doctrinal Freedom

The Christian Church's lack of a creed has been widely misinterpreted as meaning "Disciples don't believe anything." It is true that for a long period reaching far into the twentieth century, the Christian Church was in a sort of tunnel of reactionary distruct of theology. Even then, however, Disciples held specific beliefs. Today, theology—that is, systematic thought about major biblical topics such as God, Christ, the church, and salvation—is studied in Sunday church schools as well as seminaries. But I would be surprised—and dismayed—if a commission ever were appointed to write a summary statement of Christian Church doctrines to be adopted as "our position."

Actually, what the Disciples always have opposed is the use of creeds to exclude persons from the church. That happens when a person must not only confess faith but also subscribe to the particular theological formula of a denomination before becoming a member. It was this use of creeds as tests of fellowship that the Disciples' founding fathers fingered as the major cause of division among Christians. In his *Declaration and Address*, Thomas Campbell in 1809 blamed "the bitter jarrings and janglings of a party spirit" in the church on the authoritative use of "human opinions and the inventions of men." Fortunately in our day, there is much less use of creeds in examining Christians on the precise correctness of their beliefs.

Beyond the scriptural confession of faith in Jesus as the Christ and one's personal lord and savior, the Christian Church has no yardstick of orthodoxy. "No creed but Christ" is one of the Disciples' old slogans. There is no official position on such matters as the Trinity (God, Christ, and the Holy Spirit), the virgin birth, verbal inspiration of the Bible, and physical resurrection of the body. Individual Disciples have views on all kinds of theological issues, but they do not expect their opinions to be accepted by all other Christians. For many years, *The Christian-Evangelist*, a forerunner of our present journal, *The Disciple*, carried a maxim in its masthead: "In essentials, unity; in nonessentials, liberty; in all things, charity." Picked up from a saying that probably originated with Rupertus Meldenius in the seventeenth century, that proverb has been quoted in various forms throughout Disciples history. It expresses the cherished conviction that liberty should be allowed in the nonessential areas into which most creedal statements roam.

W. E. Garrison, who was a historian-philosopher with great insight into the Disciples' strengths and foibles, often spoke and wrote about the theological freedom present in the Christian Church. He felt the Disciples, who had "learned to live happily together," though "not without interesting theological disputations," gave the rest of the church "a notable demonstration of the truth that Christians who are loyal to Christ do not need to be united by theological agreement in order to be united."[7]

7. *Heritage and Destiny*. Bethany Press, 1961.

Unfortunately, legalists and fundamentalists have split themselves from the Christian Church by adopting written and unwritten tests of fellowship. It is a very un-Disciple thing to do. I already have mentioned the separations of the Churches of Christ and the independent Christian Churches, and will not dwell on those episodes here.

Variance on Social Issues

Nor do we Disciples always agree on how we should live out our commitment to Christ. As moderator of the Christian Church for the 1973-75 biennium, Jean Woolfolk wrote a pamphlet giving her characteristically direct answer to a question some Disciples ask: "Why doesn't the church stick to preaching the gospel and keep out of social issues?" But traveling to address church groups, Miss Woolfolk surely has met other Disciples who want to know why the Christian Church is not more heavily involved in solving this or that problem of society. While pietists and activists definitely are different, we believe they belong together in the church, balancing and complementing each other, and stirring up the lethargic majority in between.

My mail keeps me reminded that Disciples don't all hold the same opinion about racial justice, sexism, and other burning issues. Right now, for example, Disciples generally are committed to the alleviation of world hunger. It is a matter of first concern for many. Yet I receive letters from some Disciples who say they do not intend to do anything about hunger because the root of the problem is religious beliefs or population control practices in countries where people are starving.

James L. Merrell, editor of *The Disciple,* receives letters on more than one side of controversial issues, too. He carries many, of those letters in a column (it sometimes amounts to more than a page) appropriately headed "Response." In addition to purely religious topics such as charismatics, baptism and evangelism, letters recently have dealt with practically every concern of North American Christians: pornography, racism, abortion, foreign affairs, and capital punishment, among others. In true Disciples style, some letter-writers expressed appreciation or toleration of opposite views, wrong as they were. *The Disciple* performs an essential service in providing a forum in which readers can state their diverse opinions.

Feelings can run hot in an assembly of Disciples handling a resolution on one of those issues. When I am witnessing a verbal floor fight, however, I think back to an assembly of the Christian Church in Texas in the early seventies. All through that meeting, one man had been on his feet at a floor microphone again and again to speak against resolutions, most of which finally were passed. The thing that pleased me was that instead of resenting that delegate, the majority developed amazing understanding of him, and he of them, and he drew sincere applause from persons who opposed his views. The Design for the Christian Church (Disciples of Christ), the document we have used somewhat like a constitution since its adoption in 1968, asks individuals and congregations to express "in love any dissent" from the actions of regional or general assemblies.

Congregational Differences

There is practically as much variety among local congregations of the Christian Church as among individual Disciples. The obvious example is worship. For several years while I was a regional minister in Texas, I was a member of University Christian Church in Fort Worth and had the privilege of worshiping under the leadership of Granville T. Walker, the pastor at that time. Services usually were formal, the music of the highest quality, the liturgy meaningful, the sermon inspiring and challenging. I always left with an exultant spirit. Several years earlier, while I was regional minister in Arkansas, I preached one Sunday morning to the tiny congregation at Harrisburg. Besides myself, there were twelve present—nine women, one man, a teenage boy and a boy about ten years old. That, too, was a thrilling experience. The "church school" was one class which included all of us. The man served as superintendent and one of the women taught. After about an hour, the man stood up and said, "It's time for worship now. Let's prepare ourselves for it." Emblems for the Lord's Supper were brought to a small table on the floor level just below the center pulpit, and respectfully spread. And the service began. It was simple but it contained every element of worship. When time for Communion came, the man stepped to one side of the table, the teenager to the other, and they gave prayers. Then the teenage boy was joined by the other lad and they served the elements to the congregation (now, of course, the women might be sharing as elders and deacons).

Other differences among congregations are equally marked. There are congregations that feel they scarcely could worship without a pew-lined sanctuary, and a few that insist they never will own property. In many church schools, class sessions invariably are lecture-type expositions of Bible texts, but assorted educational techniques, including use of videotape recorders, are used in other congregations. Church finance simply is a matter of "passing the plate" in some congregations, but a growing percentage seek an annual commitment or pledge from every member. Social action runs the gamut from an occasional appeal for food and clothes for a needy family to large continuing programs in such fields as mental health, drugs, and remedial education. Almost nonexistent in some congregations, evangelism is the motivation for virtually every program in others. The right to "manage their affairs under the Lordship of Jesus Christ" is among those "recognized and safeguarded to congregations" in The Design.

Even membership policies can vary. With rare exceptions, however, the differences relate to accepting transfers from denominations that baptize by modes other than immersion. While all disciples baptize by immersion, there are "open membership" congregations that welcome Christians who have not been immersed. "Closed membership" congregations admit only persons who have been immersed or are willing to be.

Although all congregations are encouraged to give to Disciples causes, some do not. And they still are part of the Christian Church (Disciples of Christ). Financial support of general and regional programs of the church is voluntary. Nevertheless, of the 4,334 U.S. and Canadian congregations listed in the 1982 *Year Book and Directory* of the church, approximately 88 percent (3,835) felt responsible enough for Disciples-related outreach to support it financially.

With so many rights guaranteed by The Design, it never should be necessary for a congregation to withdraw from the Christian Church to protect its freedom. The persons who stampeded several thousand congregations into taking their names out of the official Disciples listing in the late sixties and early seventies simply did not tell the truth. (I reported that schismatic action in the chapter on Disciples origins.)

Embracing of Diversity

During 1963 and 1964 the Disciples' Commission on Brotherhood Restructure wrote and polished a statement called "The Nature of the Structure Our Brotherhood Seeks." I was a member and later administrative secretary of that commission, so I recall the deliberateness with which the group phrased an introduction and seven points. The fifth point, "The Brotherhood Seeks Structures That Manifest Both Unity and Diversity," said:

The brotherhood will continue to be open and inviting to congregations and agencies willing to embody, at one and the same time, the diversity and unity that characterize Christian fellowship. Where diversity is embodied, unity does not lead to conformity; where unity is embodied, diversity does not lead to divisiveness. The simultaneous expression of unity and diversity results in interrelatedness with responsibility but without the tyranny of either the minority or the majority. The brotherhood should continue to seek structures which make provision for differences of opinion, always attempting within the bonds of love to discover amid differences the unifying will of God.

When the Provisional Design was developed, the objective of assuring "both unity and diversity" was written into its preamble (paragraph 4).

We Disciples are more alike than we are different. But we are not homogenized, and do not feel the need to be. Our dream still is for a unity among Christians that tolerates, even encourages, diversity.

51

Structure

One way to explain the present-day structure of the Christian Church (Disciples of Christ) is to trace a century and a half of controversies over organization. If this were a book of history, I probably would do it that way. But important as they undoubtedly were when they were fought, those old battles seem remote and irrelevant now. So, except for briefly pointing out the sources of this and that, I intend to stick to a description of the Disciples' current structure.

In a sense, we finally have achieved what eluded the Christian Church's nineteenth-century founders—restoration of the New Testament church. Don't misunderstand me. We modern Disciples seldom call ourselves the Restoration Movement, as earlier generations did. The founders and many of their successors mistakenly thought that the New Testament offered a single pattern of church organization. That is what they felt should be restored. Alexander Campbell, whose description of the apostolic church model became authoritative, dubbed it "the ancient order of things." Biblical scholarship in the twentieth century has informed us that the early church was a dynamic movement that developed a variety of structures. What we have restored, therefore, is a biblical understanding of organization as functional and developmental. It seems obvious to us Disciples that a New Testament church is one that revises its structures as necessary to better express its nature and carry out its mission.

Democratic Monarchy

As surely as the Roman Empire affected the polity (form of government) of the early church, Jeffersonian democracy on the

52

American frontier influenced the Christian-Disciples movement. This influence was analyzed thoroughly by George G. Beazley, Jr., and other contributors to *The Christian Church* [*Disciples of Christ*]: *An Interpretive Examination in the Cultural Context* (Bethany Press, 1973). In accord with the mood of the populace, the new religious movement espoused freedom, relied on reason, placed confidence in common people and looked ahead optimistically. Even though, ironically, Alexander Campbell acquired so much clout that he often was called "Bishop Campbell," the Disciples rejected authoritative control from outside the local congregation. Their impulse was to embody democracy in a movement that would use freedom rather than coercion in unifying the church. What resulted organizationally was a special variety of congregationalism—more accurately, several varieties of congregationalism.

Because his own views on church polity developed as the movement grew, Campbell said and wrote contradictory things about structure across his long career. Consequently, it has been possible to quote him in support of diverse kinds of congregationalism. Those who, as the present-day Churches of Christ, recognize nothing beyond the congregation as church can cite the youthful Campbell. Those with the mindset of the "independent" Christian Churches, who recognize the need for a degree of cooperation among congregations, can use arguments of a maturing Campbell. Disciples have evolved a structure that can be supported by Campbell's description of the church as a community of communities in which congregations relate to one another much as individuals do in a congregation. I, for one, doubt that quoting Campbell proves anything about the particular type of polity that is best for the church in the last quarter of the twentieth century.

On the other hand, I believe that most Disciples can see timeless validity in some of the broad New Testament-based principles Campbell enunciated about church structure: that the church is one whole living organism, the body of Christ; that authority resides in the midst of the fellowship or community; that the community is more than local; that members of the body bear responsibility for one another; that "times and circumstances" will necessitate changing the church's organizations.

Above all, we Disciples agree with Campbell's insistence that "Christ's institution is a kingdom." A Provisional Design for the Christian Church (Disciples of Christ), used as a proto-constitution since 1968, described a church in which relationships are "free and voluntary" but under the absolute rule of Christ—a democratic monarchy. Paragraph 2 of the design, which deals with the nature of the church, closes: "All dominion in the church belongs to Jesus Christ, its Lord and head, and any exercise of authority in the church on earth stands under his judgment."

Provisional Design

Development of the Provisional Design took almost the whole decade of the sixties. We called the process "brotherhood restructure." It was such a strenuous, time-consuming process that many Disciples grew tired and impatient. Some were disappointed that the structural changes were not more revolutionary. I already have told about the incited withdrawal of congregations that feared restructure would take away their freedom. After the vote adopting the Provisional Design, the 1968 Kansas City assembly spontaneously broke into singing of the Doxology. It was a genuine expression of gratitude.

Still, the process of restructure was not finished. The design had to be implemented. That is the reason it was termed provisional. Besides, we Disciples had come to realize better than before that the process of change—renewal, reformation, reorganization—never should end.

I participated in the process from the beginning, first as a member of the representative Commission on Brotherhood Restructure and later as its administrative secretary. In the course of the work, I read nearly everything Alexander Campbell wrote on church organization—mostly in his periodical, *The Millennial Harbinger*. I was struck by the fact that Campbell often urged establishment of a general church organization. To him, it was "evident and undeniable" that "there is a community beyond the family, beyond the particular congregation," and that the wider community should be organized. More than a century after Campbell was calling for a representative general church assembly, I saw a churchly structure in keeping with his dream taking shape. I remember being deeply moved in the 1964 annual meeting of the restructure commission when Ronald E. Osborn declared:

> God in his providence has brought us to a day when it would seem possible to include within one structure the congregations known as Christian Churches. What then is the character of our corporate life? It is something more than a convention, far more than a policy of cooperation, far more than an association of churches. It is the church, as surely as any congregation is the church. It is not yet the whole church, but it is the church.[8]

That marked the turning point beyond which restructure was a matter of real reformation. Two years later, when the Provisional Design was put before the church for study and reaction, Granville T. Walker, chairman of the restructure commission, observed that Disciples were at the kind of "joint" at which historians would "carve history."

Many Disciples other than the 130 on the restructure commission shared in the process. Individual and congregational study of the Provisional Design resulted in numerous constructive contributions. And there was much personal conversation and correspondence, like that with William F. Carpenter, Sr., a prominent attorney in Woodmont Christian Church in Nashville, Tennessee. Our correspondence over a two-year period produced a number of helpful changes that gave balance to the design's description of the rights and responsibilities of a congregation. Even when he was not fully satisfied, Carpenter was loyally supportive of the process. That quality of involvement undoubtedly sharpened the commission's thinking and improved the design.

When the Provisional Design was adopted in 1968, there was a general assumption that a constitution would be developed. However, in 1977 the General Assembly acknowledged that "the Provisional Design has proved to be a workable document for the church and offers flexibility." It proceeded to make minor revisions, removed the word *Provisional* from the title, and determined that *The Design* would be utilized as a "working document for the Christian Church (Disciples of Christ) until such time as a need for a constitution seems to be demanded by the conditions of both the church and the world."

---

8. *Toward the Christian Church.* Christian Board of Publication, 1964.

It would be impossible for me to include the entire Design in this book. Copies are available from the General Office of the Christian Church (Disciples of Christ), P.O. Box 1986, Indianapolis, Indiana 46206. What I will do is outline the main features of the design, tell about its implementation to date and comment on some implications of the document.

As described in the design, the Christian Church (Disciples of Christ) "manifests" itself in a general (United States and Canada) organization, regions (geographic units), and congregations. Authority flows neither "from the top down" nor "from the bottom up." In fact, there is no top or bottom. "Each manifestation, with reference to the function for which it is uniquely responsible, is characterized by its integrity, self-government, authority, rights, and responsibilities," the design affirms. This recognizes that every manifestation—congregation, region and general organization—is the church but that no one manifestation is the whole church.

Relationships in the Christian Church are "free and voluntary." In the next chapter, I will discuss God's "covenant of love," which the design identifies as the bond among Disciples.

The design recognizes both a "corporate ministry" to which every Christian is called and "an order of the ministry, set apart or ordained." Ministry also is the subject of a later chapter.

General Organization

The Design gave the Disciples their first truly representative decision-making body at the general (national/international) level. It is the General Assembly, which meets every second year.

There had been several attempts, beginning in 1849, to create a representative general assembly. Plans for conventions of delegates of congregations or states even had been approved, but not put into effect. From 1917 until 1968, the Disciples had a sort of two-house arrangement in the International Convention—a committee on recommendations representative of states and provinces, and a mass assembly which did the final voting.

It still is possible for any member of the Christian Church to register for a General Assembly, attend, and speak in business sessions. But voting is limited to voting representatives. The bulk of voters are in three categories—representatives of congregations, representatives of regions, and ordained ministers with standing in the church.

Important details are spelled out in The Design. The number of representatives allowed from each congregation, for example: "Each congregation . . . shall be entitled to have two voting representatives, plus one additional voting representative for each 500 participating members or major fraction thereof over the first 500." Also procedures for introducing regular and emergency items of business. And specific duties of the General Assembly.

The General Board is a smaller (approximately 190 voting members) deliberative body responsible to the General Assembly. Meeting annually, it processes or initiates items of business going to the General Assembly and, under broad policies determined by the assembly, reviews and evaluates the general program of the church. About half of the members of the General Board are elected by regions and the rest by the General Assembly.

A forty-member Administrative Committee of the General Board meets at least three times a year. It implements policies and actions of the General Board, provides for long-range planning and coordinates activities of administrative units.

Presiding officer for the General Assembly, the General Board and the Administrative Committee is a moderator elected by the assembly for a two-year term. There also are two vice-moderators and a parliamentarian. These are voluntary (non-salaried) officers.

The top professional (salaried) officer is the general minister and president. That double title was written into The Design purposefully. It signifies that the general minister and president not only is "concerned for the pastoral care and nurture" of the church but also serves as its chief executive officer. I was elected to my first six-year term in this humbling office in 1973, and re-elected in 1979.

General organizations that carry out the Christian Church's "witness, mission, and service to the world" are called administrative units. These range from relatively small limited-purpose units like the Disciples of Christ Historical Society to large diversified organizations like the Division of Homeland Ministries. With the adoption of the Provisional Design, organizations that had reported to the old International Convention were recognized as provisional units of the church. Since then, these units have brought their constitutions and bylaws into harmony with the design, and some significant reorganization has occurred. The General Board, which oversees the Disciples' continuing restructure, has approved the principle of creative evolution for whatever additional revising is done.

Work of the administrative units will be covered in a chapter on the Disciples' witness and service to mankind.

The general minister and president and his staff plus the chief executives of the administrative units comprise the General Cabinet, an advisory group. I can testify that even though the cabinet has no administrative authority, it is extremely valuable. What it provides is informed counsel and coordination.

Regions

When the Provisional Design was adopted, the thirty-nine existing state and multi-state organizations were recognized as provisional regions of the Christian Church. They ranged in strength from fewer than a dozen congregations to several hundred.

Gradually, under the guidance of the General Board and by mutual agreement of the provisional regions involved, the Disciples are moving in the direction of more comparable regions. In 1982, the count was down to thirty-five and several were in conversation about possible realignment. The aim of this process is to assure that all Disciples congregations have the benefit of a strong regional program and adequate care through efficient use of available resources.

According to The Design, the purpose of a region is twofold—mission and nurture. At the risk of oversimplifying, we can say that mission refers mainly to the church's outward-looking witness and service, and nurture primarily has to do with the inward-turned functions of renewal, upbuilding and care. Mission has to do with work within a region as well as regional participation in a national or international program. And nurture often involves all three manifestations of the church as, for example, in providing a support system for the professional ministry.

Regions develop their own particular structures. They are free to organize "for the most effective fulfillment of their ministry and mission." But The Design anticipates that they will have assemblies "for the transaction of business by voting representatives from the congregations."

The chief administrative and pastoral staff member of a region usually is called the regional minister. Other titles currently in use include executive minister, executive pastor, regional pastor, regional minister-president, and general minister. Depending on their needs and resources, regions employ a variety of other staff members.

Most of the larger regions have geographical subdivisions called districts or areas. Some districts and areas have staff members, frequently called area ministers, who are related to the regional staff.

Congregations

Disciples congregations in the United States and Canada are listed in our *Year Book and Directory*. The 1982 annual lists 4,334, no two of which are exactly alike. Sameness among congregations is not sought by The Design: variety is assumed. In fact, the opening paragraph of the section on congregations anticipates that the Christian Church not only will have congregations "in the historic form of the local church" but also will recognize "new corporate structures for mission, worship, and service."

It would be folly to propose a uniform structure for Disciples congregations. For what size congregations would the structure be designed? Approximately 36 percent have fewer than 100 participating members, about 26 percent have from 100 to 199 members, almost 28 percent have 200 to 499 members, and only about 10 percent have 500 or more. Or for congregations in what kind of community? There still are large numbers of Christian Churches in small towns and county seats, yet some of the strongest concentrations of Disciples are in such urban centers as Cleveland, Indianapolis, St. Louis, Kansas City, Dallas-Fort Worth, and Los Angeles. Size and location merely are two of the most obvious variables. Think of others like culture, race, age, education, economics, and life-styles of the members.

In *The Congregation as Church* (Bethany Press, 1971) Kenneth A. Kuntz describes several possible patterns of organization, all of which are in use in congregations. None of the plans are recommended for any specific congregation; rather, all are offered "as suggestions from which any congregation can develop its own organization." One reason Kuntz's book has been so useful to Disciples is that it recognizes the need for structural variety among diverse congregations earnestly striving "to respond effectively to God's mission."

Although they are long and somewhat stilted, The Design's two paragraphs on the rights and responsibilities of congregations are so precise that I am going to include them here:

84 Among the rights recognized and safeguarded to congregations are the right: to manage their affairs under the Lordship of Jesus Christ; to adopt or retain the names and charters or constitutions and bylaws; to determine in faithfulness to the gospel their practice with respect to the basis of membership; to own, control and incumber their property; to organize for carrying out the mission and witness of the church; to establish their budgets and financial policies; to call their ministers; and to participate through voting representatives in forming the corporate judgment of the Christian Church (Disciples of Christ).

85 Among the responsibilities by which congregations voluntarily demonstrate their mutual concern for the mission and witness of the whole church are the responsibility: to proclaim the gospel and administer baptism and the Lord's Supper; to provide for the spiritual nurture of their members and families; to grow in understanding that the church is a universal fellowship, transcending all barriers within the human family such as race and culture; to sustain their ministers in faithfulness and honor and, in matters pertaining to relationships with them, to seek counsel from the regional minister; to be faithful in Christian stewardship, striving to share proportionately in providing the resources for the total life, work and witness of the Christian Church (Disciples of Christ); to choose voting representatives to the general and regional assemblies; and to seek to realize the oneness of the church of Jesus Christ through cooperation with other churches of the community and with present and emerging ecumenical structures.

Again and again, The Design points out the interrelatedness among parts of the body of Christ—the congregational, regional, and general manifestations.

Organization's Place

I hope that Disciples are clear about the proper place of organization in the church. It is not the church's mission to organize—the church organizes to carry out its mission. In an illuminating paper for the *Panel of Scholars Reports,* Dwight E. Stevenson showed that in the early church "organization was secondary, a tool hammered out on the anvil of necessity" (Vol. III, *The Revival of the Churches.* Bethany Press, 1963). That's the way The Design sees it too: "The nature of the church, given by Christ, remains constant through the generations; yet in faithfulness to its mission it continues to adapt its structures to the needs and patterns of a changing world."

———— Covenant ————

A member of our General Cabinet tells about having lunch with a major supplier who was sizing up the Disciples as a potential market. This supersalesman drew out the information that the Christian Church manifests itself in congregations, regions, and a general organization, each of which has freedom and authority in its own sphere. Then, dubiously, apparently thinking about his own interlocked corporation, the man asked, "But what, if anything, holds it all together?" "A covenant," my colleague answered, "nothing else."

Perhaps the most significant decision we Disciples made in the restructure period of the sixties was to recognize ourselves as a covenant church. The covenantal relationship is not new, understand. We simply have not talked much about it recently and we have not always used the biblical term *covenant* in speaking of what binds us together.

Meaningful as it is, the covenant idea is one of the most difficult to express. Feeling it is one thing. Explaining it concretely is something else. Please bear with me.

What It Is Not

I know better than to try to describe something by saying what it is not. Nevertheless, that probably is the best way to begin an explanation of the covenant. Most people need to clear their minds of several things it is not before they can grasp what the covenant is.

The covenant among Disciples is not a contract. It is not a document binding parties to an agreement. Although we have tried to express the covenant in writing, it does not exist as a legal document to be signed.

Nor is the covenant a loyalty oath or pledge of allegiance to the Christian Church. There are occasions when we Disciples publicly declare our understanding of the covenant (later in this chapter, I will provide the text of one such affirmation). But there is no official statement of the covenant to which one must subscribe in order to be a "true Disciple."

Most important, the covenant is not merely a device someone thought up to preserve unity in the church. In fact, it is not of the church's making. God originated it.

Response to God

This point—that the covenant is God's—is paramount. Against the backdrop of the long history of covenants between God and Israel stands Jesus Christ. The eyes of faith see him as God's act establishing a new covenant. When he had given a cup to his followers on the night he was to be arrested, Jesus said to them, "This is my blood of the covenant" (Mark 14:24).

What Christians do is respond to God's covenant. The proper response is love. Unlike the Hebrews' legalistic covenants, the new covenant involves no detailed listing of obligations. We meet our obligations by living in the covenantal relationship established by God and by continuing to embody the love shown to us in Christ.

Paragraph 4 of The Design for the Christian Church (Disciples of Christ) says that "as a response to God's covenant, we commit ourselves to one another." The preamble to that document, which we have used somewhat like a constitution since 1968, affirms "the covenant of love which binds us to God and one another" and declares that "we are joined together in discipleship and in obedience to Christ." So the design for our structural relationships incorporates a New Testament understanding: our love for God and for one another is a responsive participation in the covenant made known in Christ.

Mutual Dependence

The covenant concept takes seriously the New Testament image of the church as "the body of Christ" (1 Cor. 12). It recognizes the organic unity of the body. "As it is, there are many parts, yet one body. The eye cannot say to the hand, 'I have no need of you,' nor again the head to the feet, 'I have no need of you'" (verses 20-21). By God's design, the parts of the body are dependent on one another. They "care for one another. If one member suffers, all suffer together; if one member is honored, all rejoice together" (verses 25-26). To say that we are in a convenantal relationship is to say that, in Christ, we are responsible for one another as members of any living body are.

In practical terms, this means that in the Christian Church, we sense the interdependence of various structural manifestations of the body—congregation, region and general organization. These parts not only serve and support one another but also rely on one another. This relationship is described in part in paragraph 87 of The Design:

> As part of the Christian Church (Disciples of Christ) congregations share creatively in its total mission of witness and service. Equally, the Christian Church (Disciples of Christ) in its general and regional manifestations sustains its congregations through its commitment to their welfare and needs. Thus, concern for the integrity of each manifestation is shared and witness is given to the interrelatedness of the whole church.

When a Disciples congregation is seeking a pastor, it normally consults the regional minister—not because it must, but because it has confidence in his ability to give wise counsel. Regions and congregations depend on the general manifestation for such bodily functions as operating a publishing house, preserving historical materials, and producing television spots. No general administrative unit imagines that it could provide individuals regular opportunities for worship, study, fellowship, and service; congregations do that. Countless other examples of our mutual dependence could be cited.

Thus responsibility goes with the freedom we Disciples cherish. Paul put it plainly, "You were called to freedom, brethren; only do not use your freedom as an opportunity for the flesh, but through love be servants of one another" (Gal. 5:13).

Written Expressions

From their earliest days, Disciples have tried to state in writing their covenantal relationship with God and one another. A task group of the Commission on Brotherhood Restructure (I have described the work of this commission in the chapter on structure) discovered this in the mid-1960s. It found and studied a variety of covenantal statements. Among them was one written by a Missouri congregation in 1843, which began:

> We whose Names are here unto Subscribed having first given up ourselves to God through faith in obedience to our Lord and Savior Jesus Christ do now Mutually give ourselves to one another and agree to live together in a Church capacity being Built on the foundation of Prophets and Apostles Jesus Christ being the chief Corner Stone . . .

The task group's file included statements of purpose of Disciples organizations, constitutions of congregations and other documents expressing corporate obligations.

Aided by that task group's research and recommendations, the opening paragraph of the church's Design is a declaration of our covenant in Christ:

As members of the Christian Church,
We confess that Jesus is the Christ,
the Son of the living God,
and proclaim him Lord and Savior of the world.
In Christ's name and by his grace
we accept our mission of witness
and service to all people.
We rejoice in God,
maker of heaven and earth,
and in the covenant of love
which binds us to God and one another.
Through baptism into Christ
we enter into newness of life
and are made one with the whole people of God.
In the communion of the Holy Spirit
we are joined together in discipleship
and in obedience to Christ.
At the table of the Lord
we celebrate with thanksgiving
the saving acts and presence of Christ.
Within the universal church
we receive the gift of ministry
and the light of scripture.

In the bonds of Christian faith
we yield ourselves to God
that we may serve the One
whose kingdom has no end.
Blessing, glory and honor
be to God forever. Amen.

Since the adoption of The Design, some congregations have incorporated this declaration in their constitutions. Others have used it as a model or point of departure for drafting their own statements.

The covenantal statement from the design is widely used by Disciples. It is read by worshipers at regional and general assemblies. It is used on occasions when the interrelationship of parts of the body is especially pertinent—the ordination of a minister, the installation of an area minister, the dedication of a regional office building and so on. It is included as a resource in the *Hymnbook for Christian Worship* (Bethany Press, 1970), and I would encourage Christian Churches to use the affirmation as a regular or frequent part of worship.

Inexpressible Relationship

Still, as I already have said, the covenantal relationship defies adequate expression. No statement of it would be wholly satisfying to every Disciple. That's because each of us experiences the bond of love differently.

Since childhood, I have felt congregations responding to God's covenant. I sensed the tie in 1970 when, as regional minister in Texas, I watched Christian Churches come to the aid of congregations in the Corpus Christi area that had lost property to Hurricane Celia. I have experienced the covenant in a district finding ways to train lay preachers for several of its small rural congregations. As the Disciples' general minister and president, I have looked into the eyes of audiences and known that those people and I had affinity that was far greater than the communication of the moment. I have considered procedures in mission finance introduced in the seventies evidence of the covenantal relationship in the Christian Church, for they are based on mutual trust among the three manifestations of the church. I am conscious of deep covenantal sharing in the meetings of our Council of Ministers, which includes Disciples regional ministers and our General Cabinet. My appreciation for the covenantal relationship in the Christian Church continues to grow.

Other Disciples would think of different kinds of experiences. Some surely would be more personal than the examples I have mentioned. Some experiences would deal with international relationships, some with the irrelevancy of race or sex, some with bonds that compress the generations. There are Disciples who have become especially conscious of the covenantal relationship while serving as volunteers in benevolent institutions or in summer camps or in Sunday church schools. What I suspect is that the sense of covenant is most acute in Disciples (individuals, congregations, organizations) who are self-giving and weakest in those who protect themselves.

We must all not allow ourselves to think of God's covenant as a denominational thing. The small minority of us who call ourselves Disciples must avoid that. And so should other Christians. In Christ, we all are one. We are bound to everyone who confesses Christ. Let us affirm the covenant in its fullness.

Ministry

The sign out on the church lawn says "Claudia Grant, minister." On the letterhead from the regional office is the line "William E. McKnight, regional minister." A feature in *The Disciple* tells about a nurse serving in India under the Division of Overseas Ministries. Typed beneath my name at the end of a letter is "general minister and president." A man and a woman known to the whole community as an insurance agent and a realtor administer the Lord's Supper, a ministerial function in most churches. Credits on the worship bulletin include one to the associate minister, another to the minister of music. Title of the sermon is "The Ministry of the Laity."

What do Disciples mean by ministry? Are we as confused as it might appear to a person whose definition of a minister is "A preacher who has his own church"?

Servanthood

The Christian Church never has limited use of the title minister to pastors of local congregations. In fact, there was a time when a good many Disciples felt that a congregation should not have a single designated pastor.

In the words of The Design for the Christian Church (Disciples of Christ), here is an outline of our understanding of ministry:

89 The fundamental ministry within the church is that of Jesus Christ. He calls his church to participate in this ministry.

90 By virtue of membership in the church, every Christian enters into the corporate ministry of God's people. . . .

91 In addition, the church recognizes an order of the ministry, set apart or ordained, under God, to equip the whole people to fulfill their corporate ministry.

From the New Testament, we draw our concept of the ministry of Christ, his church and those set apart: servanthood.[9] The model of ministry provided by Jesus is that of a servant. So the church to which the ministry of Christ was entrusted is in the world as a servant-people. And the public or representative offices the church bestows on some of its members are servant roles.

As some other Protestants do, we Disciples talk much of the "priesthood of all believers." When we do, however, we seldom have in mind *priesthood* defined narrowly as mediation between humanity and God. Rather, that is our shorthand for speaking of the much broader ministry into which every Christian is inducted at baptism. We mean that Christ lays servanthood on the whole church and that "each Christian fulfills his own calling as a servant of Christ sent into the world" (The Design, paragraph 90).

Early in the history of the Christian-Disciples movement, this insight into the nature of ministry was distorted into anticlericalism (opposition to a professional ministry). Alexander Campbell, the most influential of the Disciples' founders, launched an attack on a hireling clergy. And frontiersmen heady with democracy, fed up with ministerial pretension and confident of their self-sufficiency, gladly joined in. Just a few years later, when the need for better ministerial leadership became obvious, Campbell tried to blunt the movement's anticlericalism and effect order. But the "anti" position had become a tradition that only time, necessity, and New Testament study by later generations would change.

There still is mild resistance by some to use of the title *reverend*, especially among Disciples who remember the church's earliest tradition. Omission of the Rev. before names of Christian Church ministers is the style of *The Disciple* and most other publications of the church. But it no longer is unusual for a pastor to be called reverend and I usually address my letters to them that way. I have noticed that it is getting easier for Disciples to refer to ordained and licensed ministers as clergy.

To be clergy is not to have prerogatives and control in the body of Christ, but to be set apart for servanthood.

---

9. Ronald E. Osborn developed this biblical exposition of ministry in *In Christ's Place*, Bethany Press, 1967.

Offices

In *The Christian System,* published and revised during the 1830s, Alexander Campbell identified three ministerial offices as "standing and immutable . . . perpetual":

> *Bishops,* whose office it is to preside over, to instruct, and to edify the community . . . *Deacons,* or servants—whether called treasurers, almoners, stewards, doorkeepers, or messengers, . . . and *Evangelists* . . . sent out into the world [to preach, make converts, and plant congregations].

Today, we would call those officers elders, deacons, and traveling preachers. Immutable as they seemed to Campbell, the only office that has not changed significantly is that of deacon.

Notice that Campbell's list of offices did not include pastors. Elders, of which there always was a plurality (at least two), carried the pastoral responsibilities. Christian Churches that called pastors were criticized by some for adopting the one-man system. By the end of the nineteenth century, however, mainstream Disciples considered it desirable for congregations to have settled pastors—if they could get them.

In its Design, the Christian Church recognizes two offices in the order of the ministry—ordained minister and licensed minister. The design also acknowledges two local offices—eldership and the diaconate—"for the performance of certain functions of ministry appropriate to the offices."

The office of ordained minister, according to the design, includes such persons as "pastors, associates, chaplains, ministers of Christian education and missionaries; teachers with ministerial standing; administrators and ministers serving the Christian Church (Disciples of Christ) beyond the local congregation and in ecumenical relationships." Licensed ministers who serve in specific situations, include such persons as workers in specialized church vocations, ministerial students, and those who have "not fulfilled educational standards for ordination but in whom the church discerns manifest gifts for ministry."

One of the needs of the Christian Church is to recover an understanding of the local offices of elder and deacon as ministerial, and restore biblical meaning to them. As it is, few elders and deacons think of themselves as sharing in the ministry. They consider themselves lay people, which they are. But they also are ministers. The Design points out that an elder has such duties as "sharing in the ministration of baptism and the Lord's Supper and the conduct of worship, and sharing in the pastoral care and spiritual leadership of the congregation." Persons elected to the diaconate assist in "the ministration of baptism and the Lord's Supper, in the conduct of worship, and in the pastoral care and spiritual leadership of the congregation." All of those are ministerial functions.

Hollis Miller filled the office of elder as faithfully as anyone I have known. He was an elder in Central Christian Church of Vernon, Texas, when I went there as a young pastor. A wholesale grocery salesman then, Mr. Miller traveled all over West Texas selling to small stores. He always called himself a "drummer." But he was something of a minister as well, never too hurried to talk with people about their personal concerns. Mr. Miller was known to make hospital calls as he traveled. And he sometimes was asked to fill the pulpit for congregations in the area. Back home, he was a teaching, counseling, leading elder—never presumptuous, but always helpful. No ordained minister ever was more influential in my own life than that local elder.

Appointment and Recognition

Self-appointed ministers are not in the Disciples tradition. The church chooses and sets apart (ordains, licenses, or elects) its ministers. In *The Christian System,* Campbell said that all the church's officers, "whether for its services at home or abroad, when fully proved, are to be formally and solemnly set apart by the imposition of the hands of the presbytery or eldership of the church." Resolution No. 3 of the Disciples' first national convention in 1849 stressed the importance of examining candidates carefully before ordaining them as evangelists and turning them loose on the church. It's a fact that some great pastors of the Christian Church never were ordained. Regrettably, it also is a fact that some congregations have been victimized by unworthy preachers with no credentials other than their own testimony to having been "called." In the main, Disciples want good order in the selection and recognition of ministers.

Current policies of the Christian Church are stated in The Design and a related document approved by the General Assembly, "Policies and Criteria for the Order of Ministry."[10]

The policy document describes an orderly process by which the church inducts persons into its representative ministry and grants recognition. Covered are qualifications for admission to the order of ministry, preparation for service, candidacy, ordination, licensing, and ministerial standing (recognition by the Christian Church). Congregations and regions share responsibility in ordination and licensing. A congregation or congregations recommend a candidate and participate in the act of ordination, which ordinarily takes place in a congregation. The region's responsibility is to establish procedures to evaluate applicants, nurture them, authorize and supervise ordination or licensing, and in the case of a licensed minister, define the area of service.

To no one's surprise, the most memorable ordination service for me was my own. But one of the most symbolic about which I have heard was that of Ann Updegraff in her home congregation in Fort Lauderdale, Florida, in December 1973. It spoke of the relationship of the set-apart ministry to the whole body. Toward the end of the service, Robert P. Kelley, pastor of the sponsoring congregation, took Ms. Updegraff to the center aisle about halfway back in the sanctuary—and left her standing there. She was glaringly alone. Soon, the congregation grasped the meaning. People began leaving the pews to stand beside the young minister as a sign of their support for her in their common ministry. It has been described to me as a very moving experience.

Certification of the standing of ministers also is a regional responsibility. Ordained and licensed ministers with standing are listed in the *Year Book and Directory of the Christian Church.*

I wish that all deeply motivated Disciples could realize that they do not have to be ordained or licensed ministers to perform significant services (ministries). That's good New Testament. And true to Disciples tradition. As a regional minister, I counseled a number of times with persons who had left secular occupations in middle age to serve the church through its public ministry. For some, that had been a wise and useful decision. For others, enter-

---

10. Copies of these documents are available from the General Office of the Christian Church, P.O. Box 1986, Indianapolis, Indiana 46206.

ing the ministry had led to painful disillusionment and even tragedy. The latter might have been more effective as elders and deacons.

Deployment

Congregations and Disciples organizations that employ ministers "call" them. Call is our jargon that can't quite be translated with a single word. It means *select* and *invite to serve* and *challenge* and *enter into servant-servants relation with* and more. The best some Disciples could do with a definition of call is "the opposite of accepting a minister assigned to us." At any rate, it's the heart of our ministerial placement or deployment system.

I've laughed with Disciples when they have quipped that it is a misnomer to speak of our way of doing things as a system. Yet it is a system. It's not perfect. Nor is an episcopal system in which ministers are appointed to their parishes. Like any other system, ours is okay for ministers, congregations, and organizations for which it works well, and horrible for those it fails. There's room for improvement.

Using a congregation searching for a pastor as an example, here is how it works.[11] The congregation forms a pulpit or personnel committee, which normally works in consultation with the regional minister. Through the regional minister, the committee has access to Minister's Informaton Schedules on literally hundreds of ministers (the committee does not consider that many, of course). The regional minister uses the Department of Ministry of the church's Division of Homeland Ministries as a clearinghouse for information schedules and names of ministers available for relocation. Systematically, the committee develops a list of prospects, investigates them, reduces the list and finally selects one minister to approach. If the committee agrees on a minister and he/she will accept a call if it is extended, the committee makes its recommendation to the congregation's official board. Action by the congregation often is required. After affirmative votes, the call is extended. Use of a "letter of calling" is recommended.

---

11. The process is described fully in a handbook by Thomas E. Wood, *The Church Seeks a Minister*. Division of Homeland Ministries, Christian Church.

Deployment is to a variety of ministries. Of the 6,706 ordained and licensed ministers listed in the 1982 edition of the *Year Book and Directory,* 2,559 were pastors. The second largest group was 1,450 retired ministers. There were chaplains, campus ministers, staff members of regions and general units, missionaries, and a dozen other categories besides those that come immediately to mind—ministers of Christian education and associate ministers of congregations.

A problem in ministerial deployment is providing preachers for small congregations that cannot pay salaries large enough to support a minister's family. Disciples elders are keeping some of those congregations alive.

Support

For more than a century now, Disciples have been trying to improve the support of the ministry, financially as well as morally. Our present Pension Fund of the Christian Church can be traced from a committee on ministerial support and relief formed in 1873. According to figures provided by the Pension Fund, the average Christian Church minister's salary increased from $2,300 plus parsonage in 1925 to $14,274 plus parsonage in 1981. Average compensation for ministers remains below that of any other professional group, however.

As a minister to ministers, I know that the support they need cannot be stated in dollars, essential as adequate pay is. They require a concerned fellowship within which to exercise their servanthood. One expression of that need was the decision of a group of ministers in 1974 to begin formation of a Congress of Disciples Clergy to provide "mutual support and concern—spiritually, emotionally, and physically." Support means friendship, provision of opportunities for continuing education, career counseling, protection against ruin after unwarranted dismissal and so on. No congregation or employing organization can offer a complete support system. Caring for the ministry is a major responsibility of regions—one in which several general units share. It's a high priority of mine.

Faithfulness to Christ's Ministry

Particularly in the Christian Church, which relies on voluntary relationships, there is little awe for any ministerial office. It is not the office to which people respond. It is the quality of the servanthood of the person who holds the office. It is the kind of life the minister lives—what William Martin Smith, president of the Pension Fund, has called "that visible rhetoric."[12] As Granville T. Walker explained pastoral effectiveness, "What he is as a man is more important than anything he does or says in the course of his ministrations."[13] That is true of ordained and licensed ministers in the order of the ministry, and elders and deacons in the local congregation. May I never forget that the church's general minister and president is not excepted.

12. Reed Lectures on *Servants Without Hire*. Disciples of Christ Historical Society, 1968.

13. *Four Faces of Christian Ministry*. Bethany Press, 1973.

Sacraments

People who know little else about us Disciples can tell you that we baptize by immersion and observe the Lord's Supper every Sunday.

Both practices were adopted by the Christian Church's nineteenth-century founding fathers in their effort to bring about Christian unity by restoring New Testament ways. As I deal with the two sacraments separately, I will cite some of the scriptures Disciples used in developing what they believed could be catholic positions.

For generations, Disciples almost always spoke of baptism and the Lord's Supper as ordinances rather than sacraments. *Ordinance* meant something ordained or commended by Christ. *Sacrament,* as it had been defined metaphysically, smacked too much of what Disciples perceived as magic. Not used by New Testament writers, sacrament seemed to convey more from the church's medieval theology than from the Scriptures. Nowadays, stripped of much of its objectional freight, sacrament is an acceptable term in the Christian Church. We think of the sacraments as symbolic acts of the church ordained by Christ in which the whole gospel is recalled and experienced anew.

There is no authoritative Disciples interpretation of either sacrament. Views differ. Yet we Disciples hold much in common from contemporary study as well as our tradition, and I will try to reflect that.

Baptism

Traditionally, Disciples have practiced baptism of believers by immersion for remission of sins. To Christ's Great Commission

(Matt. 28:19), our forefathers related numerous New Testament references to baptism. Especially Peter's instruction (Acts 2:38): "Repent, and be baptized every one of you in the name of Jesus Christ for the forgiveness of your sins; and you shall receive the gift of the Holy Spirit." And the account of Philip's baptism of the Ethiopian eunuch (Acts 8:38, 39): "they both went down into the water . . . [and] came up out of the water."

Believers' baptism has contrasted us with churches that baptize infants. Immersion in water has made us stand out from churches that baptize by sprinkling or pouring water—the vast majority.

As I already have said, the meanings Disciples find in baptism are multiple. The best I can do is mention half a dozen understandings that are current among us. Disciples still would agree with one of their founders, Alexander Campbell, that "baptism . . . is a sort of embodiment of the gospel, and a solemn expression of it all in a single act." Just as it re-presents the death, burial of the old self of the penitent believer, and the birth of a new being "in Christ" (this interpretation is well-nigh universal among us). Since the days Walter Scott, another of the founders, rode the frontier, teaching his five-finger exercise—"faith, repentance, baptism, remission of sins, and the gift of the Holy Spirit"—Disciples have linked baptism with the process of salvation. Not that immersion in water itself somehow effects reconciliation with God, but that it expresses and seals in the heart of the believer what already is occurring through faith. Disciples generally think of baptism as initiation into the church. Beyond the kind of induction of an individual that will lead to listing on a membership roll, baptism is seen as the uniting of persons in the body of Christ. A strong thread of conviction among us Disciples is that baptism is ordination to the universal priesthood (I touched on the priesthood of all believers in the chapter on ministry). Somewhere in that overview most Disciples could find the kernels of their own views on the meanings of baptism.

Disciples hold to believers' baptism because we feel that a response of faith (obedience, choice, decision, commitment) is essential. We have not baptized infants because, practically speaking, they have not sinned and because they are incapable of faith-responses. Yet, seeing the value of affirming that our children will be nurtured in an environment of faith, many Christian Churches have periodic services of dedication or blessing for young children and their Christian parents. Children reared in the church usually make their confessions of faith and are baptized when they are twelve to fifteen years old, often after a period of instruction. Honesty forces us to admit that some of our children probably make their decisions naively at the urging of adults rather than out of conviction. In the main, however, Disciples baptize only persons who have decided to respond to God's initiative in Jesus Christ.

While I was pastor at Vernon, Texas, I baptized forty-two persons—twenty-seven of them adults—following a special visitation evangelism emphasis I conducted. That may well have been the high point of my pastoral ministry. Those forty-two along with sixty others who came into Central Christian Church on the same day by transfer of membership made me feel I was in the midst of a veritable Pentecost.

Hardly anyone doubts that immersion was the form of baptism used by the church in apostolic times. The church was more than a thousand years old before sprinkling became more common than immersion in Western Christianity. Eastern churches still employ some form of immersion. But Stephen J. England expressed the opinion of many present-day Disciples when he wrote, "The fact is that antiquity is not the only—or perhaps the best—test of proper observance."[14] The real question, England continued, is the meaning of the form employed. To most Disciples, immersion is a more adequate symbol than other modes of baptism.

I remember well my own baptism at the age of 12. Ivan J. Young was my pastor then. I remember telling him that I felt like Jesus must have when he went into the water. His explanation of obedience and the symbolism of death, burial, and resurrection have stayed with me through the years.

Under The Design for the Christian Church (Disciples of Christ), congregations determine their own membership practices. This always has been so. As a result, the Christian Church has both "open membership" congregations that will accept members from any other church and "closed membership" con-

---

14. "Toward a Theology of Baptism," *Panel of Scholars Reports,* Vol. III, *The Revival of the Churches.* Bethany Press, 1963.

gregations that will admit only those who either have been immersed or consent to be.

We are facing the same issue in ecumenical circles. Baptism is recognized as a bond of unity. There is "one Lord, one faith, one baptism" (Eph. 4:5). But can divided churches bring themselves to recognize each other's members—and by implication, the validity of each other's baptisms? The term for this usually is "mutual recognition of members."

Simultaneously, ecumenical groups are taking believers' baptism and immersion seriously. For years, Disciples and other immersionists were considered an eccentric minority. A study paper issued by the Faith and Order Commission of the World Council of Churches in 1982 declares: "In the celebration of baptism the symbolic dimension of water should be taken seriously and not minimized. The act of immersion can vividly express the reality that in baptism the Christian participates in the death, burial and resurrection of Christ" (*Baptism, Eucharist and Ministry*).

For consideration of the ecumenical dimensions of baptism, the Lord's Supper and ministry, I suggest the Faith and Order Paper No. 111, and the study series on *The Covenant* produced for the conversations between the Christian Church (Disciples of Christ) and the United Church of Christ.

Lord's Supper

Weekly participation in the Lord's Supper always has been important to me—partly, I am sure, because that is all I have ever known. Disciples founders decided on the basis of their study of the Bible that the supper should be celebrated every Sunday as the central event in a congregation's worship. They read, "On the first day of the week" the church "gathered together to break bread" (Acts 20:7). Breaking of bread, taken to mean the Lord's Supper, was in a passage that nineteenth-century restorationist Disciples used virtually as an outline of proper worship (Acts 2:42). Whatever legalism there might have been in the original motivation for weekly observance has long since disappeared. I sense that Disciples consider the Lord's Supper indispensable today because it is an effective sign and assurance of the presence of Christ.

Disciples do not fit neatly into traditional categories of thinking about the Lord's Supper—we pick what seems best to us from various concepts of the sacrament. For example, we tend to think of the Lord's Supper as an act of remembrance, but we also are conscious of the real presence of Christ. Some would say that we are theologically sloppy. I prefer to believe that we Disciples appreciate the fundamental insights, though not all of the fine-spun doctrines, in most Christian perceptions of the Table.

On many of our Communion tables is carved the phrase, "in remembrance of me." We break bread and drink from the cup to remember. Yet remembrance as it is prescribed in Paul's account of the institution of the Lord's Supper (1 Cor. 11:23-26) is far more than bringing past events to mind: it is proclamation of the mighty acts of God in Christ, a recalling of the events in history in which God reconciled the world unto himself, a fresh revelatory encounter.

Explaining precisely how Christ is present never has been crucial to Disciples, so doctrines about supposed changes in the bread and wine seem rather beside the point to us. The loaf and the cup are symbols that awaken our senses to the presence of the Lord. It is his table and he is there. His presence is a spiritual reality. The name we frequently use for the sacrament, Communion, speaks of our feeling that it draws us into extraordinary fellowship with Christ and with one another.

Eucharist, the name by which many Christians know the Lord's Supper, is not even in the vocabularies of some Disciples. The meaning of the word thanksgiving always has been part of the Christian Church's understanding of the sacrament, however. We have the example of Christ from the institution of the supper, of course: "when he had given thanks [he gave the cup and the bread to the disciples]" (Luke 22:17-20). But we also can recall the entire Christ-event and give joyous thanks for that, and all other gifts from God.

Through the years, the Christian Church has held communion services during its General Assemblies. When thousands from congregations throughout the United States and Canada share the fellowship of the Lord's Supper, it is an unforgettable experience. One of the most striking impressions of our General Assembly was described by A. C. Dharmaraj, general secretary of the Church of North India: "To see these seven or eight thousands partake of the Lord's Supper, administered in about thirty minutes in pin-drop silence by about four hundred men, women and youth, was heart-ravishing, and then I said to myself, 'Surely, the Lord is here and the Spirit is moving.'"

Disciples consider the Lord's Supper open to all Christians. Usually, the bread and the cup are offered to everyone by passing them among the worshipers, row by row. If anything is said about who should partake, it is likely to be a quote from Paul: "Let a man examine himself, and so eat of the bread and drink of the cup" (1 Cor. 11:28).

Intercommunion (participation in the Lord's Supper with members of other churches) is not a problem for Disciples. We long have favored it. Therefore, the Consultation on Church Union's proposal of interim eucharistic fellowship among the ten participating churches early in the seventies seemed reasonable to us. Most Disciples would concur that sharing in the Lord's Supper across denominational lines is both a way to the goal of Christian unity and a sign of at least partial attainment of that goal.

Administration

Unlike most other churches, the Christian Church does not limit administration of the sacraments to ordained clergy. Disciples reject the notion that the validity of either baptism or the Lord's Supper is dependent on a set-apart ministry. Ordained or licensed ministers normally do the baptizing, and often preside at the Lord's Table. But lay members can fill either role, and frequently do. In fact, the usual pattern in the Christian Church is for elders to give the prayers of thanksgiving for the loaf and the cup, and for deacons to serve the elements.

Most Disciples can remember Sundays when there was no preacher, but the elders and deacons conducted a communion service. It was complete with a reading of the words of institution from the New Testament, a brief message about the meaning of the Lord's Supper, prayers of thanks and appropriate hymns. Members of tiny frontier congregations meeting in cabins celebrated that way. Youth groups and lay organizations on weekend retreats do today.

It is our experience that lay people can administer the sacraments so that these corporate acts of the church present all that faith anticipates—the grace of God.

Minorities

In 1982 the National Convocation of black Disciples honored me with a Liberation Award of which I am very proud. And although I did chair the merger committee before I became general minister and president which brought black and white conventions together into one General Assembly and I do try to be the consistent advocate of justice and equality that the award says, the "opening of doors to service and empowerment for African-Americans and other oppressed peoples" cited in the award is largely the work of racial minority peoples themselves.

For too much of our history, Disciples women and youth as well as ethnic groups have been frustrated by the assumption that those who are not white, English-speaking, adult males have little to offer. While those biases have not been eliminated, minorities have better opportunities to participate fully in the Christian Church today than ever before.

Blacks

There were black Disciples almost as soon as the movement was launched during the first decade of the nineteenth century. Both founding branches' original congregations—the Christians' Cane Ridge in Kentucky and the Disciples' Brush Run in Pennsylvania—included blacks. Alexander Campbell, the most influential founder, is said to have baptized many blacks.

Until after the Civil War, most black members of Christian-Disciples congregations were slaves. Usually, blacks attending services with whites sat apart in balconies or on back pews, or stood outside near windows. Few held offices. Robert L. Jordan, commenting on the period when "the master, the freedman, the slave, all worshiped together," observed that Disciples recognized all men as brothers "but not as equals."[15]

One of the antebellum black preachers was a former slave converted at Cane Ridge who took the name of Alexander Campbell. Freed to become pastor of the earliest black Christian Church on record at Midway, Kentucky, Campbell attended Transylvania University in Lexington and later evangelized widely in Kentucky and North Carolina. Two of his sons also were ministers.

Another former slave was the second missionary sent overseas by the Disciples. Alexander Cross, bought free and educated, went to Liberia in 1853 and died there of a tropical fever two years later.

Disciples did not split over the slavery issue into North and South churches as Baptists, Methodists, and Presbyterians did. Some say that is because the movement had no structure to divide. A better explanation is that although most Disciples leaders opposed slavery, they shunned the abolitionist position in the interest of church unity. Contending that the New Testament does not explicitly forbid slavery, they treated the issue as a matter of "opinion." The white Alexander Campbell was so intent on preserving the "unity of spirit among Christians of the South and of the North" that he seemed wishy-washy, sometimes attacking slavery and at other times almost defending it. Nevertheless, Disciples took sides. They fought for the Confederacy as well as the Union. Authors of the most recent history of the Disciples conclude that "they suffered an actual if not an official split."[16]

After emancipation and the war, formation of black congregations accelerated. At first, the work was done mainly by individuals, sometimes with the support of white congregations and state conventions. Later, missionary organizations joined the effort. With separate congregations came black district and state conventions, and in time a national organization.

15. *Two Races in One Fellowship*. United Christian Church, Detroit, 1944.

16. Lester G. McAllister and William E. Tucker, *Journey in Faith: A History of the Christian Church (Disciples of Christ)*. Bethany Press, 1975.

A black who had a hand in these developments was Preston Taylor. Born a slave, he became a minister and finally a successful businessman, and for generations was the key figure among black Disciples. In 1878, when he was a pastor at Mt. Sterling, Kentucky, Taylor helped form the first lasting national organization of blacks, the National Convention of the Churches of Christ. He was appointed national evangelist to work among blacks for the American Christian Missionary Society in 1883. Three years later, Taylor settled in Nashville, Tennessee, where he served as minister of Gay Street Christian Church before starting a funeral, cemetery, and recreational park business. Through the years, Taylor contended for a share of leadership for blacks in the white-controlled missionary societies working among his people. Convinced by World War I that a stronger black convention was needed, Taylor called a meeting for August 1917. He was elected first president of the resulting National Christian Missionary Convention, which continued until it was merged into the general structure of the Christian Church in 1969. Taylor's legacy of valuable property in Nashville enabled his interest in development and empowerment of black Disciples to survive his death in 1931.

The obscurity of the black Alexander Campbell, Cross, Taylor, and scores of other notable leaders has left gaping holes in Disciples history. Hopefully, that can be corrected under the guidance of a Black Disciples Historical Materials Committee of the National Convocation of the Christian Church (I will identify the convocation below). This committee is working closely with the Disciples of Christ Historical Society. Appropriately, a 1976-77 study of black Disciples, published by the Christian Board of Publication for use by the Christian Men's Fellowship and Christian Women's Fellowship, was called *The Untold Story*.

Part of that story is the constructive work done by general missionary agencies of the church. True, whites have tended to be paternalistic in relating to blacks, not only in the nineteenth century but right up to the present. But the mission boards made solid contributions, not the least of which was in the field of education. An outstanding example is Southern Christian Institute (Mt. Beulah) near Edwards, Mississippi. Opened in 1882 on a plantation, SCI provided schooling for many of the men and women who became Disciples stalwarts. In the mid-fifties, SCI was merged into Tougaloo (Mississippi) College, a school founded by Congregationalists soon after the Civil War. Another example is Jarvis Christian College at Hawkins, Texas. Now an accredited four-year college, it began in 1912 as an elementary school. Biographical data sheets of a number of present-day Christian Church leaders show that they attended Jarvis.

But the day of the missionary approach to blacks is behind us. We are moving toward wholeness in the church.

With the blending of the National Christian Missionary Convention into the restructured Christian Church (Disciples of Christ) in 1969, a National Convocation was created as a forum for black concerns. The convocation's administrative secretary is an assistant to the general minister and president. In its biennial meetings, the convocation airs issues, brings black interests to the attention of the total church, provides fellowship and training experiences, and nudges us Disciples toward real inclusiveness.

A 32-member Committee on Black and Hispanic Concerns reviews and gives advice on plans and programs of the Disciples' general units and regions. To cover all of the significant progress that has been reported to that committee recently would require another chapter. But one example is a leadership development project for black and Hispanic ministers in New York and New England. It was sponsored jointly by the Division of Higher Education and the Northeastern Region, and funded by the Board of Church Extension. Another example is the Division of Homeland Ministries' program to recruit black candidates for the ministry and subsidize some pastors' salaries. Still another was black radio spots produced cooperatively by the communication offices of the Christian Church and several other denominations. And yet another, the calling of more blacks to regional staff positions.

During the 1971-73 biennium, the Christian Church's highest elective post, moderator, was filled superbly by a black, Walter D. Bingham. Pastor, scholar, and ecumenical leader, Bingham was widely acclaimed for his patient, pastoral leadership of the whole church as well as his own congregation, Third Christian Church of Louisville, Kentucky. Another black, Mrs. Carnella J. Barnes of Los Angeles, was president of the International Christian Women's Fellowship for the 1974-78 quadrennium.

Representation of blacks on boards, committees, and delegations of the church has improved during the past decade. So has employment at general and regional levels. The church's target, set in a resolution of the 1969 General Assembly, is 20 percent in both categories.

Greatest needs of black Disciples, as identified by the National Convocation, are (1) ministerial recruitment and leadership development, (2) strengthening of existing congregations, (3) establishment of new congregations, and (4) membership growth.

Precise statistics are not available. But there are approximately 50,000 members in about 550 predominantly black Christian Churches in the United States besides the blacks who belong to predominantly white congregations. That is about 4 percent of Disciples in the U.S. and Canada.

Hispanics

The first congregation of Spanish-speaking Disciples in the United States was organized in 1899 in San Antonio. It was a project of the American Christian Missionary Society. To too great an extent, the Christian Church has continued to treat Americans of Hispanic descent as inferior mission objects rather than as worthy constituents.

After three quarters of a century, we Disciples have twenty-eight Spanish-speaking congregations with approximately 2,500 members, two community centers serving Hispanics, several Anglo congregations with Spanish departments and a few scattered mission projects, some operated by local congregations. Ecumenically, we are involved in ministries to migrant farm workers, day-care centers, and other such service programs. That's about it. Disciples achievements plainly do not measure up to the opportunity we have had. I agree with Lucas Torres, former director of the Division of Homeland Ministries' office of program services to Spanish and bilingual congregations, that Disciples need to "move toward the masses of unchurched Spanish Americans in the United States in a well-planned, massive program of Christian witness and service." David A. Vargas, current program services director and vice-chairman of the Black and Hispanic Concerns Committee, is leading in that direction in a significant way.

A major reason for the relative ineffectiveness of Disciples has been the Anglo majority's lack of real understanding of Hispanics. Most of us, for example, make the erroneous assumption that all people who speak Spanish have a common heritage. In actuality, the estimated 15 million Hispanics in the United States include those whose ancestors inhabited the Southwest before English-speaking people arrived as well as those whose roots are in Mexico, Puerto Rico, Cuba, the Dominican Republic, and various other Latin American countries. While it is true that most Hispanics are counted as Roman Catholics, only a small percentage attend mass regularly—a fact no one can assess easily, especially in an ecumenical era. Sticking with our "melting pot" image, we usually have acted as though a prime objective of the church was to free Hispanics from their own culture and Americanize them. We Anglos have a lot to learn. Disciples who want a quick but enlightening introduction to Hispanic Americans should read Torres' book for Christian Men's Fellowship/Christian Women's Fellowship group studies in 1975-76, *Dignidad* published by the Christian Board of Publication in 1975.

Most Hispanic Disciples are in two regions, the Southwest (Texas-New Mexico) and the Northeast (New York-New England). The rest are sprinkled across the country, primarily in urban centers like Miami, Chicago, Kansas City, and Los Angeles.

In the Southwest, Hispanics mainly are Mexican Americans (native Americans of Mexican descent and immigrants from Mexico) though pastors of Christian Churches there are from varied backgrounds—Mexican, Cuban, Puerto Rican, Nicaraguan, and Argentinian. A Spanish-speaking convention there functions as an integral part of the regional organization of the Christian Church in the Southwest, and Hispanics participate fully in district/area as well as regional activities. An increasing number of congregations are becoming bilingual.

Hispanic Disciples in the Northeast are mostly from Puerto Rican stock. Many are first- and second-generation products of a great revival that swept through Christian churches on the island of Puerto Rico in the 1930s. As they migrated to New York City, Puerto Ricans brought with them their zealous brand of Christianity that is strong on warmth, evangelism, and stewardship. Their first congregation was La Hermosa (the Beautiful) Christian Church. Started shortly before 1940 in an upper Manhattan apartment, La Hermosa now is housed in a building on 110th

Street across from the north edge of Central Park. As in the Southwest, Hispanic Disciples in the Northeast have a convention linked to the church's regional organization.

Inman Christian Center in San Antonio, founded in 1913, is an exemplary community service institution. Directed by Daniel H. Saucedo, who grew up in the neighborhood, Inman provides day care for children, remedial teaching, clubs, camps, recreational programs, health and nutrition services, medical and dental clinics, citizenship classes, counseling, and so on. Younger but with a strong community development program is Eastmont Community Center, which serves Mexican Americans in East Los Angeles.

Hispanics are represented in deliberative and administrative bodies at the general level of the Christian Church and in regions where there are significant numbers of Spanish-speaking congregations. But Torres said in *Dignidad* that "Hispanic Disciples want more participation in the decision-making process." By 1982, five Hispanics were serving on the church's General Board, two of those elected to the forty-member Administrative Committee as well.

Disciples held a National Strategy Conference on Hispanic Ministries in June 1975. Approximately seventy participants grappled with problems that affect Hispanics—poor housing, poverty, inadequate education, language barriers, cultural shock, racism, and so on—and developed findings and proposals to be referred to appropriate program units. Among the needs are funds for church establishment and development, training for ministerial and lay leadership, printed materials in Spanish, and increased opportunities for Hispanic input.

Spanish-speaking Disciples seem committed to the concept of oneness in the church, but they are determined to preserve cultural plurality (Hispanic ways along with Anglo ways) and to be accepted as equals. In 1980 they began holding a biennial national Hispanic convention, bringing together the various Hispanic elements on the off-year of the General Assembly so as to meet both commitments.

American Asians and Native Americans

There are fewer numbers of American Asians and Native Americans in the Christian Church than blacks and Hispanics but they are beginning to make their voices heard. Korean and Filipino congregations meet in Los Angeles as well as Korean congregations in Chicago and Libertyville, Ill. The American Asians have organized under such leadership as that of David Kagiwada in Indianapolis and Grace Kim in Los Angeles.

Resources for Reconciliation

In the late sixties, the Christian Church launched its Reconciliation program to cope with racism, poverty, and other problems contributing to America's crisis in human relations. Violence was ripping at the cities. Fed-up minorities were making demands of institutions, including the church, that brought backlash. I can testify that having blacks and Hispanics in the church helped Disciples deal with the crisis constructively. The minorities became living resources for Reconciliation.

I will say more about Reconciliation in the upcoming chapter on witness and service. But this is the place to pay tribute to the roles black and Spanish-speaking Disciples have played. Dollars could not buy what their presence has provided during recent troubled years.

Women

Women probably never have been a numerical minority in the Christian Church. In the opening paragraph of her book about Disciples women and their ogranizations, Lorraine Lollis quips that it is the story of the "better half" of the church and adds, "Although we would not necessarily disavow any controversial interpretations of the term, 'better half' might merely denote a simple numerical majority."[17] Of the 6,976 persons registered for the 1981 General Assembly, 3,668 (53 percent) were women. I suspect, but can't prove, that an even higher percentage of Sunday morning worshipers in congregations is female.

Yet women have been treated somewhat like a minority. During much of the Christian Church's history they have not been adequately represented in decision-making bodies at any level. Few women have held high offices, either elective or staff. Even

---

17. *The Shape of Adam's Rib.* Bethany Press, 1970.

today, only a handful of ordained women are pastors. That is improving. And congregations gradually are switching over to a male-and-female "diaconate" just as most elect women as elders.

Disciples women always have found ways to get around barriers to make their contributions. In 1874, when the male-dominated American Christian Missionary Society was floundering, Caroline Neville Pearre led in the formation of the Christian Woman's Board of Missions. That is when Disciples got serious about the Great Commission (Matthew 28:18-20). Besides sending and supporting missionaries on four continents, CWBM started a variety of outreach enterprises in the homeland. Among them were educational institutions and service centers for minorities (examples: Inman Christian Center, San Antonio; Jarvis Christian College, Hawkins, Texas; Hazel Green Academy, Kentucky) and Bible chairs related to great state universities (Michigan, Virginia, Kansas, and Texas). In 1910 the women opened the College of Missions, the first graduate-level school for training missionaries, in a building still used for our general offices in Indianapolis. Total receipts of CWBM in 1919 were $691,950. The next year, the women's organization merged with other Disciples agencies to form The United Christian Missionary Society. Two years later, women's missionary societies and circles provided more than half of the total receipts of the UCMS. Even with the changes that have occurred in outreach giving in the past half century, Christian Women's Fellowships are credited with nearly 20 percent of the total Basic Mission Finance giving of the church.

The idea of a quota system to provide proportionate representation is somewhat repugnant to many. It goes against the grain with those of us who believe leadership should be based only on qualifications. However, the facts are that positions of leadership are hogged by white males. Because the Christian Church's General Board has proposed guidelines of one-third laymen, one-third laywomen and one-third clergy (both men and women), nominating committees are paying particular attention to proportionate representation. Out of 519 positions on the General Board, administrative unit boards, committees and commissions, 174 (33.5 percent) were filled by women in 1982. Jean Woolfolk, the church's first woman moderator (1973-75), also became the first woman chief executive of a general administrative unit, serving as president of the Church Finance Council from 1976 until her retirement early in 1983. She was a leader in ecumenical circles as well, representing the Disciples at the National Council of Churches (U.S.A.), Consultation on Church Union, Berlin conference on sexism, and as an American member of the Central Committee of the World Council of Churches. A Little Rock attorney and insurance executive she helped pave the way for another Little Rock woman executive, banker Joy L. Greer who served as moderator of the Disciples in 1981-83.

At any given time, as many as half a dozen women serve as moderators of their regions. Cynthia L. Hale, a North Carolina prison chaplain, became president of the National Convocation of the Christian Church in 1982 while still in her 20s. Two Disciples women, Mildred Baltzell of Dallas and Eunice Santana de Velez of Puerto Rico, have served as vice-presidents of the National Council of Churches in recent years.

Youth

Youth representation also is on the upswing. Young people are serving on boards, committees, and official delegations of congregations, regions, and the general organization. There are students on both the General Board and Administrative Committee, for instance. More than 8 percent of the membership of the 1982 General Board of the church was youth, two were high school students, twelve were in college and two in seminary. More than 800 students have registered at General Assemblies, a third of them voting representatives.

One of the most to-the-point floor debates of the 1975 meeting of the General Board was among youth. The subject was a proposed "Covenant of Opportunity" by which a congregation or a region could commit itself to the goal of seeing that no Disciples youth would be prevented by finances from attending a church-related school. I have observed equally effective participation by teenagers in regional and General Assemblies.

Parts of One Body

We Disciples are misunderstanding the minorities among us if we hear their rhetoric as separatism, racism, sexism, or radicalism. What they are saying is that they want to belong to a whole church in which the worth of each part is recognized. They are telling the church that it needs what blacks, Hispanics, other ethnic groups, women, and youth have to offer. I sense that the rightness of that is dawning on us and that gradually the Christian Church is becoming a truly inclusive fellowship.

—— Witness and Service ——

One of my responsibilities as general minister and president is to know what the Christian Church (Disciples of Christ) is doing. I try. But hardly a day passes without my learning of another area of ministry of one of our eleven administrative units, thirty-five regions, or more than 4,300 congregations in the United States and Canada. Or a program of which I had not been aware at a Disciples-related educational institution, home mission center, or social and health service delivery point. Not to mention the scores of ecumenical ministries through which the Christian Church witnesses and serves.

Change accounts for much of the difficulty of keeping up. Work of the church is transformed under such diverse internal and external influences as shifting priorities, new attitudes of foreign governments, an improved ecumenical climate, "white flight" from the cities, more representative decision-making bodies, the tendency of people to live longer, and the competition of tax-supported community colleges.

Not even the Disciples' *Year Book and Directory*, which annually is almost an inch thick, presents the whole story. The most I can hope to do in a few pages is to indicate the scope of the Christian Church's outreach.

General Units

At the general (national/international) level, administrative units "meet responsibilities of the Christian Church in its witness, mission and service to the world" (The Design for the Christian Church [Disciples of Christ]). The principal administrative units are classified as either divisions or councils, though some have neither word in their names. I will present those units in alphabetical order, giving a short paragraph of information on each.

Board of Church Extension assists congregations and church-related organizations in planning and financing facilities. Services include general counseling on overall strategy for building projects, guidance on research and planning, leadership for fundraising, loans for new property or improvements, and investment plans. Besides facilities for congregations, Church Extension helps with such projects as construction of college buildings, development of campgrounds and erection of office structures. With an admirable record of response to actions of our General Assemblies, this unit has led in such areas as investing in minority-controlled financial institutions and providing interest-free loans to certain inner-city and minority congregations.

Christian Board of Publication is the Disciples' editing, printing and merchandising unit. It publishes books (this one, for example), curricular materials for Christian education, and a number of periodicals, including the church's official journal, *The Disciple*. Besides its own products, the Christian Board markets books, other resources, and church supplies from other manufacturers. A major undertaking in the mid-seventies was participation in what might be the largest-ever ecumenical partnership in curriculum development—Christian Education: Shared Approaches. In this project, a number of denominations planned and published materials cooperatively. Strictly nonprofit, the publishing house allocates its surplus earnings, if any, as grants-in-aid to various Disciples programs.

Christian Church Foundation receives gifts to benefit the whole church, manages accumulated permanent funds and distributes income from those funds. A gift added to the foundation's permanent funds produces earnings that either are divided among causes of the church or given to the specific causes designated by the donor. It is possible for a gift to produce income for the donor for life, then support the work of the church. Foundations services range from confidential counseling on estate planning to management of permanent funds on behalf of a congregation. The foundation is expected to have a key role in implementing a development program that will support all parts of the church—congregations, regions, institutions, and general units.

Church Finance Council receives and distributes gifts in support of practically everything we Disciples do outside our local parishes. Successor to Unified Promotion, which did similar work until 1974, the finance council also helps congregations with programs of stewardship development and every member commitment. Contrary to a widespread misconception, the council does not decide how mission finance funds will be used: a Commission on Budget Evaluation elected by the General Board and unrelated to any organization makes the allocations to general units and educational institutions, and recommends the level of support of those causes from the regions. National (U.S.A. and Canada) and World Councils of Churches also receive gifts through the finance unit.

Council on Christian Unity has been introduced briefly in the chapter on the Disciples' unity ideal. This council carries the full-time assignment of not letting the Christian Church forget its commitment to unity. It is the council that guides our ecumenical relations, administers Disciples participation in church union conversations and encourages study of issues involved in Christian unity. One of the most significant services of this unit is publication of a quarterly, *Mid-Stream: An Ecumenical Journal,* which long has been a resource for ecumenists in all churches. For a number of years, *Mid-Stream* has contained major documents of the Consultation on Church Union, for example. Unlike most other units, the Council on Christian Unity has paid memberships.

Disciples of Christ Historical Society maintains a library, archives, and research facilities in the Thomas W. Phillips Memorial in Nashville, Tennessee. Materials of other branches of the Christian-Disciples movement—the Churches of Christ and the independent Christian Churches (see the chapters on our identity problem and origins)—as well as those of the Disciples are collected and made available. The society is as concerned about preserving valuable materials of congregations as about serving as the archival agency of the general organization of the church. It has helped congregations prepare histories and furnished writers private carrels for research. The Historical Society's membership dues include a subscription to its periodical, *Discipliana.*

Division of Higher Education links the Christian Church with its own institutions and the public sector of higher education. Its services are directed both toward the church and toward the board's thirty-six member institutions—eighteen colleges and universities, four graduate seminaries, three seminary foundations houses, two seminary associates, and nine specialized institutions. One of the division's roles in relation to Disciples schools is that of convener, bringing together persons who do similar work—directors of field education in seminaries, for example. Programs include cooperation with nine other denominations in United Ministries in Higher Education (campus ministry), administration of student financial aid, and enlistment of students for ministry.

Division of Homeland Ministries strengthens congregations by recommending programs and providing resources, and involves us Disciples in diverse ministries across North America. With the Christian Board of Publication and the Church Finance Council, this division produces *Vanguard*, a program journal for congregations. Six departments are Christian education, church in society, church women, evangelism and membership, church men, and ministry. In addition, four home mission centers—All Peoples Christian Center, Los Angeles; Hazel Green Academy, Kentucky; Inman Christian Center, San Antonio; and Yakima Indian Christian Mission, Washington—are supported. In the 1980s, one of the literally hundreds of activities of Homeland Ministries was to have helped more than 2,000 refugees from countries around the world relocate in the United States.

Division of Overseas Ministries is the unit through which American and Canadian Disciples witness and serve in partnership with Christians in more than two dozen other countries. In the chapter on the ideal of unity, I mentioned this division's commitment to ecumenical effort. Overseas Ministries operates under a policy adopted by the General Assembly of the church, in which not only ecumenical style is specified but which requires that the work be done as partners with indigenous churches and councils of churches rather than in a one-way mission flow as managers. The 1981 policy also commits the division to place special emphasis in working for, and with, the poor and oppressed. Overseas Ministries tries to respond to our sister churches' requests for the personnel they need—educators, agricultural technologists, public health administrators, communication experts and social workers as well as pastors and persons skilled in training church leaders. Success stories could be related from more than two dozen countries. Among them is that of Rajanikant and Maybelle Arole, a husband-and-wife medical team, whose success in training paramedics in the villages of India has caused the World Health Organization to rate theirs as one of the nine most important experiments in public health in the whole world.

National Benevolent Association is our organization for delivering social and health services to dependent/neglected and handicapped children, youth, older adults, the ill, and the mentally retarded. As it has since the St. Louis Christian Home for children was opened in 1889, the NBA operates home centers. But the unit's programs of care have been diversified in recent years. There now are retirement centers where older adults take maximum responsibility for themselves, learning and residential centers for the mentally retarded, foster care and adoptive placement services, family counseling, convalescent hospitals, an alternative school for youth not making progress in normal schools, and programs to assist congregations and other organizations in their own ministries.

Pension Fund not only operates the Disciples' pension system for church employees but also administers gifts for ministerial relief and provides supplementary services. Sound management of investments has made possible special apportionments of earnings to increase contractual pensions and pension credits. Benefits have been hiked in recent years, as often as possible, without an increase in dues. Among services added during the past decade is a health-care insurance program. Gift money enables the Pension Fund to make supplemental gifts and relief grants to those on the "low" or "no" pension rolls, offer gift memberships to seminary students, provide emergency aid to ministerial families, and render such other services as interim ministerial placement information and personal finance counsel.

Other units at the general level are Christmount Christian Assembly, a leadership training facility on a 640-acre site in the Blue Ridge Mountains of North Carolina; Disciples Peace Fellowship, an organization of individuals focusing on the cause of world peace and such related issues as hunger, conscientious objection to war and children's rights; European Evangelistic

Society, which operates a center for scholarship at Tubingen, Germany; National City Christian Church Corporation, which holds and manages property used by a Disciples congregation in the heart of Washington; and National Evangelistic Association, an organization for promoting this central task of the church.

The General Office (office of the general minister and president) is not a program unit. But it does provide several services. These include publication of the *Year Book and Directory;* operation of research, legal and communication offices; and administration of the General Assembly, General Board, Administrative Committee, National Convocation (see the chapter on minorities), and a number of committees and commissions.

Over-and-Above Ministries

In response to acute human needs and emergencies, the Disciples have created two special programs that are carried out through various Christian Church, ecumenical, and secular organizations. Both rely on gifts over and above basic mission finance. Neither has a program staff.

One is the Week of Compassion, the Christian Church's participation in the ecumenical One Great Hour of Sharing. Largely in special offerings collected during a February observance, Disciples give more than $2 million a year to deal with hunger, disasters such as floods and earthquakes, refugees, and other global problems. Much of that work is done through Church World Service of the National Council of Churches (U.S.A.) and the Commission on Interchurch Aid, Refugee and World Service of the World Council of Churches.

The other over-and-above ministry is Reconciliation, which began as the Disciples' response to America's crisis in human relations in the closing years of the sixties. It is a program to effect reconciliation by combatting poverty, injustice, racism, and other divisive forces. Projects funded by a general Reconciliation committee and by regions range from development programs for children of low-income parents to formation of co-ops among the poor. There are day-care centers, schools for teaching marketable skills, legal aid for minority persons enmeshed in litigation, action to relieve domestic hunger, community improvement efforts, and a variety of other projects. Special offerings taken in the fall plus through-the-year gifts have been running well over $400,000 a year.

Higher Education Institutions

Listed alphabetically, the eighteen liberal arts colleges and universities that are members of the Disciples' Board of Higher Education are Atlantic Christian College, Wilson, North Carolina; Bethany (West Virginia) College; Chapman College, Orange, California; Columbia (Missouri) College; Culver-Stockton College, Canton, Missouri; Drake University, Des Moines, Iowa; Drury College, Springfield, Missouri; Eureka (Illinois) College; Hiram (Ohio) College; Jarvis Christian College, Hawkins, Texas; Lynchburg (Virginia) College; Midway (Kentucky) College; Northwest Christian College, Eugene, Oregon; Phillips University, Enid, Oklahoma; Texas Christian University, Forth Worth; Tougaloo (Mississippi) College; Transylvania College, Lexington, Kentucky; and William Woods College, Fulton, Missouri.

The four Christian Church seminaries are Brite Divinity School of TCU; Christian Theological Seminary, Indianapolis; Graduate Seminary of Phillips; and Lexington (Kentucky) Theological Seminary.

The three Disciples foundation houses associated with seminaries that are not related to the Christian Church are Disciples Divinity House, University of Chicago; Disciples Divinity House, Vanderbilt University, Nashville; and Disciples Seminary Foundation, School of Theology at Claremont, California. Two institutions have a "seminary associate" relationship. They are the Evangelical Seminary of Puerto Rico at Hato Rey and the Yale University Divinity School, New Haven, Connecticut.

"Specialized institutions" include: Christian College of Georgia (at Athens); College of the Bible of Churches of Christ of Australia, Glen Iris; College of Churches of Christ in Canada, Guelph, Ontario; College of Missions, Indianapolis; Cotner College, Lincoln, Nebraska; Department of Ministry, Associated Churches of Christ in New Zealand, Dunedin; Illinois Disciple Foundation, Champaign; Kansas Bible Chair, Topeka; and Missouri School of Religion, Columbia.

Regions

In the chapter on structure, I referred to a Christian Church region's twofold purpose—mission and nurture. How a region goes about those tasks depends on a lot of factors. Peculiar needs of the field of mission, for instance (programs of the Northeast region must be pertinent to New York's dense minority population while Florida must cope with a continuous influx of new residents). The kind of nurturing given congregations and ministers is determined by regional sociology (predominantly rural or urban, communities close together or far apart, and so on) as well as "religious" considerations.

Most regions major in helping congregations secure ministerial leadership, supporting the clergy, training lay leaders, giving youth growth experiences and addressing particular human needs through action projects. Increasingly regions are using ecumenical organizations for both mission (campus ministries, planning of new congregations, and so on) and nurture (career counseling, audiovisual libraries, and so on). Regions call on the Disciples' general units for specialized services—the Board of Church Extension to counsel a congregation planning relocation, for example.

Wholeness in Outreach

Every two years the Church Finance Council brings together teams of general administrative unit leaders, representatives of the higher education institutions and executives of the regions to conduct outreach educational conferences in more than a hundred locations around the United States and Canada. Thousands of Disciples engage in this "Sharing in Mission." An audiovisual produced for one of those series was based on 1 Corinthians 12, which emphasizes the interdependence of the parts of the church. I say "Amen!" to that.

———— Mark-making ————

What do the editor of *Good Housekeeping* magazine, the coach of the University of Kentucky basketball team, and my wife have in common? They all are members of the Christian Church (Disciples of Christ).

What does the International Telephone and Telegraph Corporation (ITT), the Congress of the United States and the Parliament of Canada, and every general unit of the Christian Church share? They all have received unsolicited advice from Disciples groups concerned about social issues.

The point is that, for its size, the Christian Church has considerable visibility and quite a lot of influence.

Prominent Disciples

John Mack Carter, editor of *Good Housekeeping,* author, and former editor of other prominent women's magazines since the early sixties, is an involved member of the church. He has chaired the board of the Christian Church Foundation, served on the Communication advisory committee, spoken at General Assembly and represented Disciples as a director of Religion in American Life.

The Kentucky basketball coach, Joe B. Hall, is a member of Crestwood Christian Church in Lexington. His quintet was beaten in the 1975 national collegiate championship game by a team coached by another Disciple, John R. Wooden, who was winding up the last of his many winning seasons at the University of California. Los Angeles (UCLA).

My wife, Wanda, was a member of the Christian Church at Yale, Oklahoma, when I was the student preacher there.

National City Christian Church, strategically located on Thomas Circle in Washington, displays huge stained-glass windows in memory of two Disciples who served as President of the United States, James A. Garfield and Lyndon B. Johnson. Actually, three Disciples have been President. Ronald W. Reagan graduated from a Disciples-related college, Eureka in Illinois, and continues his affiliation with a Los Angeles Disciples congregation even though attending the Presbyterian Church. Garfield, who once was president of Hiram (Ohio) College, a Disciples-related school, was the only preacher who ever occupied the White House.

Among other Disciples who have been in the public eye: J. Irwin Miller, the Columbus, Indiana, industrialist who from 1960 to 1963 was the first layman to serve as president of the National Council of Churches (U.S.A.); Poets Vachel Lindsay and Edwin Markham, both socially conscious; and Carry Nation, the hatchet-wielding temperance leader at the turn of the century.

As I said in the chapter on the unity ideal, Disciples long have been leaders in the ecumenical movement. To name any would be to slight scores.

Corporate Influence

ITT said prominently in its 1974 annual meeting report that in response to a challenge from the Christian Church, it was making available documents relative to its activities in Chile. The corporation had been widely criticized for allegedly offering funds to influence an election in Chile. And Disciples units, following recommendations by a special task force on corporate social responsibility, have joined other religious groups in exerting influence on corporations in which they hold stock.

General Assemblies and regional gatherings of Disciples frequently have sent heads of government and lawmakers resolutions expressing their views on great issues confronting humanity. From the 1981 General Assembly, for instance, actions on limiting nuclear arms, making peace with justice a church priority, reiterating the evils of racism, decrying unethical promotion of infant formula abroad, calling on Disciples to conserve energy, and supporting self-determination for El Salvador.

Units of the church regularly receive recommendations from plenary bodies that review their work and make policies.

Do resolutions do any good? Answering that question while she was moderator of the Christian Church (1973-75), Jean Woolfolk observed, "One cannot ignore the judgment of a majority of several thousand people, even if they are not the whole 1.4 million people [in the Christian Church]." American Christians, including Disciples, have been credited with helping to pass the civil rights legislation of the sixties.

I do not intend to digress into bragging. Individually and corporately, Disciples have left their marks—and should continue to do so.

———— Future ————

Up to now, my main purpose has been to describe how the Christian Church (Disciples of Christ) looks to me in the early 1980s, with just a smattering of history to suggest how we who call ourselves Disciples got this way. As might be expected, I am not entirely satisfied with the result. I can think of too many things that have been omitted. Maybe you have been stimulated enough to want to know more. If so, read *Journey in Faith: A History of the Christian Church (Disciples of Christ)* by Lester G. McAllister and William E. Tucker (Bethany Press, 1975).

But what about the future? In the midst of thinking about the Disciples' identity, I can't help remembering the words of Lewis Carroll: "Said Alice to the Cheshire cat, 'Which way shall I go?' Said the cat, 'Where do you want to go?' 'I don't really know,' answered Alice. 'Then,' said the cat, 'if you don't know where you want to go, it doesn't much matter which way you go, does it?'" Which is to suggest that the Disciples' identity and their future— who we are and where we are going—are interrelated.

Where we want to go is to full unity of all Christians in one church. In the chapter on the Disciples' unity ideal, I pointed out that this is our distinctive reason for existing, our true identity. It is our ultimate goal. The future of the Disciples will be linked with any major movement toward church union and closely related to most ecumenical enterprises.

Along the road to that ultimate objective, we Disciples face the obligation to be obedient to the gospel and to witness to the great concerns which have characterized our history. In the inaugural issue of *The Disciple*, Ronald E. Osborn summed up what I think we might look for in the future when he reminded us that true ecumenism is not indifferentism, and cataloged matters to which our immediate attention ought to be directed. He said Disciples need to stress the centrality of Jesus Christ and the significance of confessing him as Lord; engage seriously with biblical doctrine and renew our heritage as a people of the Book; understand the biblical doctrine of the church and emphasize the meaning of the sacraments in its life; give leadership and support to efforts toward reconciliation among Christians and throughout society; recover an evangelism that communicates the Christian message in convincing terms and draws people to commitment; bear witness to freedom and diversity; and apply "churchly pragmatism" in settling such problems as inequities among minorities, delinquency and crime, development of community, the life of prayer, and witness to outsiders.[18]

For a while, Disciples gave an inordinate amount of time and effort to organization and structure. At its best, the motivation for restructure was to clarify and lift up a self-understanding that draws us as a people toward obedience. In the process, we set forth a vision of the Christian Church (Disciples of Christ) as the servant of God, a community of the spirit taking institutional form within the realities of history, a people of the covenant. At its worst, restructure was a "tinkering with machinery." The future will see still further changes along the lines I described in the chapter on structure. And that's not bad; The Design calls for "continual renewal and structural reform." A General Board task force is charged with seeing that happens.

The future ought to see us Disciples expanding our understanding and living out the meaning of covenant. In the chapter on covenant, I said that I regard the recognition of ourselves as a covenant church to be the most significant development in the restructure period. As we engage in our mission of witness and service, our relationships as parts of the church—congregations, regions, general organizations—are based on our commitment to one another in response to God's covenant, not coercion. Our relationships are free and voluntary, but we are learning that we are interdependent and that no part of the church cuts itself off from the rest in making its decisions. The future surely will find Disciples continuing to affirm that God's covenant binds them

18. "A New Start in the Journey of Faith," *The Disciple*, January 6, 1974.

not just to each other but to everyone who confesses Christ. Under the new covenant in him, Disciples of Christ will seek to manifest the life of obedient followers learning what it means to walk in God's way.

That's why we call ourselves Disciples.